FLY WITH ME

One Woman's Leap into a Life of Love and Joy

TERESA MARTIN

Cover Design & Illistration: Whitney Bruce Martin
Interior Designed by: Dishongh Scavo Barte

Printed in the United States of America
Published by Braughler Books LLC., Springboro, Ohio

First printing, 2021

ISBN: 978-1-970063-91-2

Library of Congress Control Number: 2021905969

Ordering information: Special discounts are available on quantity purchases by bookstores, corporations, associations, and others. For details, contact the publisher at:

sales@braughlerbooks.com

937-58-BOOKS

For questions or comments about this book, please write to:

info@braughlerbooks.com

Braughler™
Books
braughlerbooks.com

DEDICATION

This is for the only person who didn't get a chapter of her own
— Gertie. You are my Sage, guiding me from your Heaven.
My transformative process would never have begun without you.

ROWING ON THE LAKE

Highland Lake, Illinois 1974
Gertie and I row to shore.

I ORIGINS
MOTHER • FATHER • TWIN

II CHOICE
PARTNER • SEX • BABIES

INTRODUCTION

"What's Your SuperPower?" the kindergartner yelled while jumping off the side of the pool, dousing me from head to toe. I was left dumbstruck, by the pure honesty in her question. I was in awe that she had asked me THE question of 2020. I felt the Goddess twinkling her eyes and enjoying the humor in that moment. A little girl in pigtails and yellow floaties, whom I had just met, inserted her wisdom right into my lap and into my life.

Like any average adult, I chuckled. Chuckled at the idea that SuperPowers are real. That SuperPowers are unique to each of us. That SuperPowers are the solution in these crazy times of uncertainty. But the question lingers. A little girl in pigtails asked me the question that won't get out of my head. What. Is. My. Super. Power? Somewhere, deep down inside of me, when it's early in the morning before the sun shines through the shades, the question remains strong, in the foothold of my soul.

In the middle of the night, my Grandmother awoke me from a deep sleep. This doesn't sound concerning. Until I tell you she's been dead for twenty-six years. I couldn't "see" her, but she stood right there next to my side of the bed, waking me up like I was late for school. She nudged me, with a firmness that only grandmothers use, and said, "write poetry." Write? Poetry? It wasn't even six o'clock yet.

Grandma's firm nudge was clear. "Start writing poetry and it better be personal. REAL personal." Poetry? What in the hell was my dead grandmother doing in my kitchen adding extra cream to my coffee before the sun comes up? Instead of shaking my head, taking two Tylenol, and heading back to bed, I decided to play ball. It was Sunday, there wasn't anything to do – we were in lockdown. I wasn't tired anymore. So, hell, ok, let's open the laptop and see what happens.

What unfolded was a collection of poetry and prose that has allowed me to find the answer to the little girl's question: "What is my SuperPower?"

Each poem and its accompanying prose guided me inward, deeper, and deeper into myself, to discover burdens, mistruths, and obsessions that no longer serve me. And to say goodbye. Goodbye to limiting beliefs about myself. Goodbye to relationships that don't serve my passions, purpose, and sense of self. Hence, I sign off many poems with "Take Care," meaning "God Be with You" (goodbye), and I hope that you take care. My goodbyes tell myself and the world it is time for me to leave, and move toward a life of my choosing.

Each poem has allowed me to go outward, further and further, into the world of the unknown to discover joys and passions to guide me into my future. A future filled with purpose. "Creating art," which for me has been poetry and prose, has been the catalyst of my own transformation into a woman. A woman who is exponentially happier and fulfilled in every way, every day. I live in abundance with positive love and light all around me at work, in my marriage, as a mother, financially, in friendship, and every day, just walking the dog with the sun on my face.

What is my SuperPower? My SuperPower is my ability to go deep inside my mind and regard all the beauty and the beasts that reside there. I may reckon with this knowledge and I may decide to change it, at any time. I can change my thoughts, my beliefs, my feelings, and myself into a person of my choosing. I have the power to improve myself, my relationships, and my world into the joyful place of my choosing.

My dead grandmother knew I was not happy. With any of it. My grandmother already knew I could create a world of my choosing. Last year, she told me to "write poetry." I don't ever remember her reading one bit of poetry. But for my entire life, she told me I could do anything. Be anyone. I could even fly. "Creating" has allowed me to say goodbye to my beasts, hello to my beauty, and create a world filled with joy, where I can fly.

Fly with me.

I

ORIGINS

Mother • Father • Twin

The act of regarding, rewriting, and, ultimately, reauthoring my past has been a deeply healing experience. I have found forgiveness of self, forgiveness of others, and hope. I have hope that a beautiful life and future are possible, for all of us. Every draft of every poem, every line, brought me just a little bit closer to knowing myself deeper and making conscious decisions to transform into the person I want to be. A person who is open to receiving light and love. A person who believes she is worthy of light and love. A person who freely shares her light and love. These poems and prose were hard, really hard, to write. But write I must, if I am to fly.

·

MOTHER

·

MATTER-OF-FACTLY

For our mothers and the souls who know breast cancer

She told us there, in her sacred place, of the breast cancer

describing screenings, stages, and symptoms in soliloquy.

She offered no olive branch to her future, just silence.

Matter-of-factly. No emotion from an emotional woman.

Hospitals spoke with white coats and masks

rattling facts and figures to be decoded in our minds.

She stood there silently, asking no questions

of these medicine men.

Matter-of-factly. No emotion from an emotional woman.

Surgeons sewed the stitches that held her together

cutting into her sense of self, her insides.

She recovered, knowing no complications of the body.

Matter-of-factly. No emotions from an emotional woman.

Scars reflected in the mirror for years to come,

reminding her of betrayals.

The breast heavy and tugging

at her arm, like a tantrum about to happen.

Take Care,

of my mother,

her emotions,

matter-of-factly.

First Printed by Cordella Magazine 2021

TRADING IN MY OLD BELIEFS

I remember playing "teacher" and grading my mother at the age of 7 or 8. I gave her a "D for Deficient." She wouldn't get my brother's hearing corrected. She just kept taking him to the same doctor over and over and his hearing never got better. In my haste to play grown-up, I decided, "well, if I want something to happen, I'll have to do it myself." My brother even let me examine his ears with an otoscope. Providence prevented me from puncturing his eardrum. However, I declared, "You can hear, even the crickets. You're cured!"

I remember staring at my mother who had bandages wrapped around her wrists when I was the age of 9, knowing that she tried to kill herself. I also knew that my brother did not fathom this truth. He thought she accidentally cut herself. I remember telling my brother a partial truth, "she's really fragile and not tough like we are. We're going to have to protect her and make her stronger."

I remember Mother's infectious excitement after she was hired for her first job when I was around 13. Her first job made real money – enough to make her independent from her ex-husband. I told myself, "I don't care if she's gone all the time and only talks about work." I was at an age when I convinced myself I liked it this way – with very little supervision and even fewer questions. Even when the house became big, empty, and cold, I tried to bring warmth by cleaning, washing, and yelling out to my brother in the yard, "time for dinner! Mac N Cheese!"

When I was 23, I remember watching Mother spend money, in ways that I was not accustomed to – ways that felt foreign. She left my shabby apartment in the avenues of San Francisco for a year to travel the world. She bought me an expensive knife before leaving. I remember thinking about the scars on her wrists and angrily musing, "The only thing I have to cut in this apartment is myself."

I remember listening to Mother tell me the story of my birth, during my first pregnancy at 32. She cringed, scrunched up her face, talked about how "back then" she was knocked out for three days, received 144 stitches, and was exhausted with not one, but two babies to take care of without bottle warmers or nannies. I was profoundly shaken at the idea of my birth and thought, "How did I get cast in the lead role of the villain before I even took my first breath?"

These were my stories about "Mother" that played over and over in my head. I wrote a poem for every memory. Every poem forced me to go further. I uncovered how each memory was deeply ingrained and remained trapped in the thinking of a 7, 9, 13, 23, and 32-year-old's mind. When I took each memory out of their boxes and regarded them in the full light of day, I had found an important truth. These stories ultimately reflected more about the author, me, than Mother. My younger self had been holding onto these stories without the benefit of reflection, or knowledge, that time and experience brings. And my older self had not gone back and helped my younger self rewrite the story into one they both could understand, learn from, and let go of. Once I started writing, Mother started to become Mom.

The poem I wrote about Mom's bandaged wrists follows. I am recapping the experience from the point of view of my 9-year-old self. And I can now insert myself as I am today, in the ending. I am able to acknowledge how the infectious sadness in our home was a heaviness pinning me down. A weight that I can try and lift, now that I know it's there.

SKINNY MOTHER

For the children who nurse

She came home

bandages on both wrists.

She came home

tailored tops sliding off thin shoulders.

I hugged her fiercely from worry.

She almost broke in half,

such a twig she had become.

Shadow of her former self.

We were told by someone, I don't know who,

"you must make her a chocolate milkshake."

Triple scoop, extra chocolate syrup.

Light on the milk. Thick is best.

She needs thickness.

Milkshake medicine works.

Hint of a person, buried

under dense covers of sadness.

I only order a shake

when I feel a memory

that brings a heaviness,

an old friend, to the table.

Take care,

of my mother.

Oh, Chef,

in the Kitchen of Life.

After the first draft of this poem, I could ask myself the critical question: How do I lift the weight of sadness, the sense of responsibility, the urgency to just do something, that permeates my very bones? I thought long and hard about Mom. It dawned on me that I wasn't replaying any other stories about her in my head. There was more to the Tale than sadness, despair, rejection, fear, and self-centeredness. This was a woman who survived a nasty divorce and breast cancer. This was the woman who got on a train and left our small town for the big city with nothing but hope and a prayer that she could pay the mortgage. This was the woman who found love for herself and a new partner. This is the woman who continues to fight for her son's life even when he gives up. This woman has strength, courage, and perseverance, of epic proportions.

Time to start writing new stories. New poems.

HOUSE-MOUSE TURNED HEROINE

For Mom

House-mouse suburban new divorcee
weighing in at 98 pounds of love-loss,
puts on makeup, a new outfit,
and gets on the train.   The "city train" -

takes her out of the country-bumpkin, small-minded,
ever-dominated-by-her ex-husband-town, and straight
to the big city of Chicago. Exhausted with contentment -
smile on her face that only a working woman can know.

Every day she rode the train, gained weight,
grew confident in her step, and did it all over again.
Even though another day of not knowing
if her son is alive or dead. Her only son.

Her little boy who she read to every night.
Her strength to get on the train, every day.

A Heroine.

She becomes.

A FINAL NOTE TO MYSELF ON ITALIAN MOTHERS

First and foremost, get the recipes. Get her at a weak moment. Just in case she dies (and most Italian mothers won't die before 100), we'll always have "real" food. Food is her life. She continues to show my boys and me that food brings us together with all our senses, around a table of love and grace. Teresa — remember to fall back on food, especially if all else seems to be failing. Keep expressing gratitude before sharing a meal with the people you love, every day.

Second, don't be afraid to watch the matriarch age. An Italian woman, and I suspect every woman, gathers a force of spitfire strength from inside her old bones that no one can mess with. I've watched her chase a burglar right out of her house, I kid you not. She had that young man running scared. There is no force greater than a pissed-off old lady. Teresa — don't be afraid of aging. You aren't getting frail, you're just getting your game on.

Third, let her have her Jesus. It may not be your Jesus, but let her have it. That was a hard one for me — the Catholic-School-Girl-turned-Agnostic. But something really beautiful happened when I stopped cringing as she lit candles for every special occasion. A spirituality came into my life. A spirituality of my choosing. It has made all the difference. It whispers to me, lifting my soul ever higher. Whispers to me that yes...

I can fly.

UNEXPECTED JOY WITH MOM

Santa Fe, New Mexico 2019
Mom and I at a dog park on Christmas Day with Billy and
Harley.

·

FATHER

·

MY CHAMPION WEARS A SKIRT AND CARRIES A BOOK

For T, my younger self

Oh champion, my champion, where art thou –

maybe you were caught up, on highest bough.

Did you forget your duty, your cause, your lady,

maybe, the directions were not clear to you, come lately.

Never mind, oh champion of women, from times past –

maybe what we ladies really need, is to be aghast.

And say, if my Champion were to wear a skirt,

carry a book, and not be such a flirt.

She'd show up on time. Have my best interest in mind –

instead of making lots of noise and battle cries that bind.

What if my Champion were to wear a skirt, carry a book,

gaze out at the stars with a dream-like look.

She'd bring the strength of all the armies,

all the saints, behind us, with us,

and into our hearts, without complaint.

She'd come quietly of hoof, with her book of wise

gathered from women in different lands,

knowing no compromise.

With a heart pure of song, and a soul open to all,

she comes to our country, across our rivers,

climbs our wall with strength of hope,

to find our faith and love spoke.

As our champion, with a skirt and a book, she arrives.

CONFUSED, EMBARRASSED, ASHAMED, ANGRY, AND EVENTUALLY, FREE TO RIDE MY WAVES

Standing by the bathroom sink, I could smell the strong menthol scent of shaving cream as I heard the hiss of the canister foaming soft, white, creamy lather. Dad would put a bit on my nose with a mischievous smile. He'd shave with a towel wrapped around his waist, steam running in rivulets down the mirror. I hold this moment close. It was a time when nothing was out of the ordinary. My father was my champion. There was no danger, no embarrassment, no shame.

As I grew up, Father started to make sexual innuendos that, at first, only confused me. What did he mean when he said I looked like a boy? What did he mean when he called my butt, my "ass?" What did he mean when he cracked a joke about a hooker? Later those innuendos became more pointed. Pointed at my breasts, my "ass." The meaning no longer confused me. It was clear. Now I was mortified, embarrassed. So embarrassed that I became ashamed of my body, which was changing at such a rapid rate. My father regarded me not as a daughter, but as an object. What was I doing wrong? I tried to desperately hide inside my sweatpants, behind my brother.

I ran away to college to escape the sexual words he used in my presence. Only to return home for the summer when he got drunk and tried to get into bed with me. He was naked. Don't worry, I kicked his butt to the floor — I was in my prime and he was drunk as hell. I was very good at dealing with his "drunkenness." I had been "dealing with it" for years. But I held that particular memory inside, without telling anyone else, for so long. Long enough to let it fester, to become infected with anger, to plant a seed of hate. When I sat down to write poetry for the first time, this was my first poem. It surprised even me. But it let me bring my truth into the light. Into the light to heal.

BRAVE GYMNAST

For my sisters on and off the matte

Far away in a deep sleep,
Front door opens and closes.
Footsteps shuffle clumsily down the hall.
Ruffling, cuss words,
Thumping of shoes being discarded.

The door opened and in the light of the moon,
Stood drunk naked father.
Panic sirens sound.
Confusion twists and turns.
Dread presses down, too heavy to hold.

As he climbed into the bed,
Her far-away voice clears the confusion,
"Wrong room." She vaults over him
Onto the floor with the strength of focused intention,
Only an athlete can know.

He crawled away. Panic sirens sound.
Confusion twists and turns.
Dread presses down, too heavy to hold.

Take Care,
of small feet, as they stick the landing.

FROM A PLACE OF ANGER, TOWARD FORGIVENESS

The morning of my wedding day, I stepped into the elevator, alone, to stay out of the groom's sight. But the elevator stopped and my Father got on with his wife and my college roommate. He took one look at me and said, "Don't I make you horny?" On. My. Wedding. Day. The lump in my throat threatened to choke me. My roommate's mouth hung open, no words coming forth. My stepmother looked down at the floor, the fires of shame running up her neck. I looked away from him. Shoved that question deep down in the small box of hate, infected with time, and turned away from my father for many, many years.

In my opening statement at my first therapy appointment shortly after returning from my honeymoon, I said, "I'm not sure what to do. My father asked me if he makes me horny. On my wedding day." Six years to work that out. I never talked to my roommate about it, even though we shared four years of our lives together. Shame buried me, inside myself. Never talked to my stepmother again either. They divorced while I was on my honeymoon.

Writing a poem to capture all the emotions that swirl inside my head about my relationship with my father is impossible. But write something, I must. If I am to rewrite my story. My first poem paid homage to fear. My second, anger. These emotions are strong inside of me. Writing poetry has given these thoughts less power over me and instead allowed me to live more comfortably with their presence. I now consciously tell my anger and fear, "stay on your side of my head." You are no longer invited to every occasion."

A BAD BET

For the poker player in heels

Poker face like no other,

hiding all the rage, as he

inserts himself,

into her space

creating a cage.

He blusters and bluffs

bad bet story of old,

cards are dealt,

he pushes an air of power

'you better fold.'

Poker face like no other,

she sees his bet

pushes the pile of chips

close enough that he can feel

smooth round edges caressing fingertips.

Never knowing her poker face,

rehearsed since she could smile,

could clear emotion from her face,

her heart,

her every mile.

Dealer calls, cards turn, chips fall from grace,

in slow motion

neatly stacking in front of her poker face,

hiding all emotion.

Take Care,

of the bets you make

the women,

you try to break.

Writing this poem brought me a new insight, one that was buried heavily. The insight into the relationship between sex and money. And how it's truly about power. Power over others. I was able to come to terms with this and talk about "money" for the first time. Ever. I had to write about money and continued to remind myself to not edit it out of the final draft. My former self would have edited this out, to keep the peace. I must be honest with myself, even if I am alone in my truth.

My father asked me to sign over my rights to "bank stock" when I just arrived home from the hospital, exhausted with a newborn and toddler. I have no idea what the deal entailed. I just knew that I couldn't listen to another phone call from Dad saying, "I need you to sign those papers... the money wasn't really meant for you....it's my money...the family would want it this way... you're just lucky you got that fancy private school paid for... you don't need any money..." I was sick and tired of the whole thing and couldn't be a part of it. As I faxed over the papers, I said out loud to an empty office, "Here are your damn papers, signed."

I walked away from an unknown amount of dollars and cents, but I do know that it gave me what I wanted more than anything. The freedom to walk away from him. I made the decision. I signed the papers and I walked away. My brother followed my lead like he always does when it comes to "Dad." If my brother resents me for leading him down that path, he's never said. The only mention we make to each other with a knowing look, is, "we don't owe the old man a damn thing."

My father is old now. He can hardly walk. He needs to be taken care of in every way — toileting, showering, feeding, transporting. The list goes on and on. He floats in and out over the phone from sensical to nonsensical speech. No force behind the words. No life behind the meaning. Yet, I do not feel sorry for him. I do feel loss though. The loss that I never knew my only sister because I walked away from "father." In my mind, she was a part of a packaged deal given she was almost 30 years my junior and a small child when I walked away from my father. I missed her birthdays, basketball games, and graduations. All those things I hated my "Dad" for missing.

I own my decision and take responsibility. I understand now that the biggest consequence of my infected relationship with my father is how it impacted my decision-making in regards to the rest of the family. I'm not proud of walking away from my entire family to "get away" from him. I know now, I can only hurt myself and while doing so, hurt my brother, my sister, and my family. Every day, I choose to walk away from hurting myself with pent-up anger, resentment, frustration, unfulfilled wishes of having a father, and, especially, the jealousy I feel over the other girls who have fathers. I watch these thoughts and shepherd them right on through, so they don't sit and fester. It's a lot harder than it sounds. Often, I take to writing. If I can "see" the feelings on the page, I can hold them in my hand like a sculpture. I can turn them around and look at them from different angles, figuring out how to make these feelings take up space differently in my head.

I've found through my poetry that it's not about forgiveness. It's about releasing harm, from inside my sense of self. It's about loving myself and reminding myself that some people do not love, or do not love in a way, that makes any sense to me. I am my own Champion. I can love myself with my whole heart and replace hurtful thoughts and actions with healing thoughts and actions.

I tell myself "I Love You" every night looking deeply into my own eyes in the mirror. It sounds crazy as hell, but the "mirror" exercise is a great place to start when your self-esteem has sunk to an all-time low. It took me nine nights before I could even look myself in the eye. But now, I look, I say "I love you," and I mean it. And I'm so grateful for this powerful way to connect with myself. So grateful.

Continually reading my poetry out loud has shown me the power of repeating words. Positive words are nourishing. Expressing positive words has become my habit now. I express gratitude every single day for marrying the most loving man on the planet, for having the most loving brother any young girl could have ever had, for the possibility, no matter how small, to regain a sister one day. Gratitude. Everyday.

A FINAL NOTE TO MYSELF ON WALKING TOWARD LIFE

Teresa — Separating from Dad is a long and sequential series of emotions. Separation is not fast. Separation is not a clean break. Separation is slow, steady, small footsteps, of every day, of every year, moving toward who you are and what you want. You're walking toward your life. Keep praying and meditating for what you want, for where you are going. And remember how you have learned to define "prayer." According to someone unknown to myself, "Prayer is not asking for what I want, but asking to be changed in ways I can't even imagine."

I pray every day for my brother and sister. I envision the three of us at the beach, surfing together. Riding the waves filled with dolphins jumping out into the light, showing us how to play together, with joy in our hearts.

I pray every day that my father finds his peace, and love in his heart. I pray that he loves his wife and young daughter in a way that he cannot with my brother or me. I pray that his family forgives me for walking away from them. I pray to find a relationship and love with my father's family again.

SURFING TOWARD MY LIFE

San Diego, California 2020
Me trying out a loaner board.

•

TWIN

•

THE PRODIGAL SON HAS A SISTER

For Wendy who Yearns for Neverland

Off he went, my brother,
to a place called Neverland.

He needs to make his mark,
his mark upon the world.
He needs to find himself,
his place among the men.

The rumors can't be true,
about the place he's gone
where wild men
abandon the rules,
never to return again.

We will wait and speculate,
on all the great things he has done,
raise him to the clouds where,
Sages and Saints of daring feat,
do not know where the intersection
of land, and Never meet.

Now you, little Missy, you stay put,
in this place called house and home.
You need to see to our needs you see,
our needs, above your own.
You need to offer yourself, you understand,
your place is not among the men.

The facts are true, so listen close,
about the life you'll lead,
where true women follow all the rules,
staying silent 'til the end.
Society will wait and speculate,
on the misdeeds we have saved you from,
keep your feet firmly planted here
knowing your place,
the place that we call home.

We wait and wait, here at home,
for the Son to return.
Return from Neverland,
with tales of conquest,
love, courage, fate.

As the son returns,
we see
where
he's really been.

So long, farewell,
and God be with you,
says the sister to everyone,
as she walks out the door
leaving behind,
the Prodigal son.

First read for the Mental Health Association of San Francisco 2021

I DREAM OF MY BROTHER, THE "BOUNCER," AT THE GATES OF HEAVEN

My twin brother, Dave, wanted to be a sports announcer when he "grew up" — he loved watching the games. Any game. He knew stats on players and teams that impressed even the most hardened of coaches. He felt the pressure to play the game, instead of talk about it, though. It's not easy to look like an athlete, be physically gifted, and come from an athlete's family. He became the defensive tackle, small forward, catcher, and under-ten handicap golfer. And above all, Captain. Captain of every team he ever played on. The quiet, strong, fair-minded Captain.

He could improvise just about anything you threw his way, too. He could turn anything into something funny. Once as we were unloading groceries, I tossed a peanut butter jar at him to put away. The jar was endorsed by Peter Pan of Neverland. Our beloved Peter, from our favorite story. Dave caught the jar one-handed, and sang, "Peanut, peanut butter, and Jelly. Peter's got the peanuts, got the peanuts, got the peanuts. Peter sold his peanuts, sold his peanuts. Peter sold out the Wonder, sold out the Wonder, sold out the Wonder. Peanuts... peanut butter and jelly." At age 11, Dave was already the most insightful and funny person I would ever meet.

We are "twins" — for fifty-two years now people have asked us if we are "identical." Really? I'm a girl. But what they meant was how we were "in sync" as kids. Our childhood was filled with the two of us running around the driveway, swimming out to the raft, playing catch until we couldn't see the ball, and sneaking up to the roof to jump into a snow pile. We moved together silently. We knew what the other was going to say, going to do, going to get in trouble for. A quick glance was all it took and we'd know what the other was thinking. I didn't know our "twin thing" was so powerful. Until it was gone. Alcohol and drugs claimed my twin, leaving me to bear witness.

Alcohol and drugs stole the Dave I knew. He could no longer control his thoughts and emotions. It was all rolled up into a biting, acerbic, diatribe. Somehow it was my fault that he never got married, didn't know his son, didn't finish college, wasn't able to keep a job. I didn't "believe" him. But I knew in my heart, that he believed himself. An even worse fate. In his mind, he wasn't stretching the truth or lying or placing blame elsewhere. He was speaking his truth. His truth, his mind, his ability to think, his emotions — they all changed. Transformed in ways that I could no longer recognize or understand. His explosive temper has kicked out more doors, walls, people than he will ever be able to repair. But underneath the addiction is a boy, my brother, my twin. I tried to capture both the idea that my brother has changed, and stayed the same, despite the disease of addiction with this next poem. It has helped me truly regard the complexity of the disease and how I can feel conflicting emotions when it comes to his behavior.

IT'S ONLY

For every Captain, who sails in her tears.

I was the Captain on a large ship,

sailing the world, looking for treasures.

My first mate, my brother,

feared the sea. He feared the water.

Oh Aquarius, my twin feared the water.

It was Electric, his fear.

His Words to his Captain,

"We can't do that,

it's not safe

it's too deep,

it's too dangerous."

His Captain's Orders,

"It's only a mast to climb.

It's only an ocean to swim.

It's only a sailboat to sail.

It's only a deck to repair."

It's only. It's only.

Many years later, his reply to his Captain,

"It's only a few drinks.

It's only a few shots.

It's only a chaser.

It's only one next round."

It's only. It's only.

Take care,

of "hello-my-name-is" brother,

who fears the open sea.

WHAT DOES A JOURNEY OF A SISTER LOOK LIKE, WHEN HER TWIN IS DIAGNOSED WITH AN ADDICTION?

It starts with admitting a problem exists, and you have no solutions. In my case, it started with sitting my parents down to tell them just that – "Dave is addicted to alcohol and drugs and he needs help." And over the next 15 years, they continued to accept and deny the conversation ever happened. I have had to bring them back into reality, and out of denial. When mom says, "Oh do you think Davey will ever get married?" I have to be the one to say (omitting all exasperation), "I don't know Mom. Dave doesn't even seem to have a place to live right now, and is trying hard to just take care of himself."

Of course, his addiction has changed his relationship with his friends. He has new friends whom I do not know, he has lost many of his old friends, and his life can not be compared to any of his friends old or new. Once upon a time, he had wonderful friends who said in all earnestness, "Let's all get together in Phoenix and do an intervention so he goes to rehab." And over the next 15 years, I witnessed how rehab can and cannot help him. More heartbreaking, I watched him lose a friend with every passing year – maybe he owes them money, maybe he got ugly with them, maybe… During my last visit with him, I gently asked him "how is so-and-so." He looked at me with blank eyes for a minute – like he didn't even know his closest friend from high school.

Every day as I scroll through social media, I see his friends' lives, filled with love and laughter. Their joy puts Dave's reality in stark relief. This physically pains me. I am so grateful to see how many of his friends did not fall into the abyss with him. Most of the time, though, I am so incredibly angry that he fell into the abyss. Alone. And I refuse to follow him.

The abyss of addiction is filled with lies and worse, lies of omission. In my case, it involves having someone ask me in casual conversation, "How's Dave's son doing in Kentucky?" My mind reeled, "He has a son?!" As "the sister," it was my duty to tell my Italian mother that she has a grandson. A grandson who is not "on the way," but has been fully arrived for fourteen years.

My nephew. A young man who I couldn't be prouder to know now. A young man that has shown me how to love Dave, without judgment.

The lies of addiction always involve money. Lots of money. It is further exacerbated by divorced parents who don't agree on anything. "That damn kid [Dave] blew his entire college fund." Still hearing that one. I'm not sure what they expected when they handed over a lump sum of "college money" without any rules or regulations to a boy in his twenties. On the other hand, as a girl, the strictest of rules and regulations were made very clear – we will pay for college tuition and your apartment. Period. And those grades better be A's. Period. And you have to work all summer, every summer. Period. No fancy unpaid internships for you, little Missy. Who do you think you are, asking to intern at the Great Barrier Reef? Waiting tables. That's what you'll be doing. Period. Period. Period. Privilege is a funny thing. It can be equal parts helpful and hurtful – for both Dave and me.

And finally, addiction is inside a family – it permeates our dynamic. It is spending Christmas dinner in a conversation revolving around your brother, who is missing in action again this holiday season. He is gone, to wherever he goes. Yet, he still becomes the focus of the dinner conversation, "Have you heard from Dave, is he ok, where is he?" Each holiday season, I continue to have no answers.

This is what the journey looks like as a sister of a twin who has a disease called addiction. Grappling with anger, resentment, and frustration has defined adulthood for me in more ways than I am comfortable admitting. So, what did I do? I escaped. A very child-like defense – run, hide, hope that time and miles will take care of the demons. My weak attempt to escape did not address what I had created in my head.

While I did my best to shield my husband and sons, "addiction dynamic" permeated my reasoning and beliefs. It has influenced my own family and how I am as a mother. I find myself wanting to control everything – especially anything I consider as possibly "unsafe." Worse yet, I deem myself as the only one with enough sobriety and sanity to deal with a situation when it gets out of control. Not a good look when you're surrounded by competent, caring, put-together people.

The "addiction dynamic" has influenced me in many ways. I'm quick to judge. I'm quick to assume. And I'm quick to walk away. About everything. If I don't change this, it will be my ultimate undoing. It's time to change. Time to dig deep and improve how I think, feel, and believe about people, family, and relationships. Change it. Really change it. I had no idea where to start. I found a book by Jack Canfield and the first chapter said, "take 100% responsibility for everything." My initial response was "Are you F$%^*@* kidding me?" But then I started writing poetry.

The poems showed me I am responsible, not for Dave, but for my thoughts, beliefs, and behaviors. Taking "responsibility" is not "saving Dave," it's holding myself accountable for my every thought, belief, action, and emotion. This is hard. Hard as a rock. Hard as hell. But take responsibility I must. Not for Dave's life, but for the record that keeps playing over and over inside my head.

I now know life is an "inside job" – literally and figuratively. If I want answers, solutions, change, it's got to happen inside of me. This is not easy for me – at all. I now crave writing, to uncover alternatives, to rewrite the draft of myself, to find a new way forward toward an ending of my choosing. I have to get up every single morning and remind myself that I am not my thoughts. I am the person who hears them, while still questioning and changing them. I can ask myself, "Really? Are you really the only person in this situation who can handle it? Are you really the only sane person in the room? Are you really responsible for everyone's shit?" I can take myself off my own pedestal. I can look around, eye to eye, as opposed to my "higher than thou" position of authority, and ask, "How in the hell are we going to handle this one?" Sharing an experience with others instead of putting myself above them, and honoring each person's contribution, especially in sticky situations, is creating so much more joy in my relationships and, not surprisingly, better solutions.

Not only can I question my sense of authority and judgment, but I can, instead, focus on what creates joy at the moment, brings calm to my tummy, deflates those wrinkles that scrunch on my forehead. I can create more smile lines. I can laugh. Instead of getting bogged down in my negativity, I can give an unexpected call to an old friend and just tell her she's great. I can give my husband a pinch on the booty, just because. Worrying and obsessing about Dave gets me nowhere. Being "in control of everything" gets me nowhere. But finding joy in the relationships that are right in front of me, right now, makes all the difference.

However, there is one thought that has been the hardest to change about my brother. Every time I find out he's "off the wagon," I begin to write and rewrite his eulogy. I've been doing this for so long, I wasn't even aware of it until the "eulogy" ended up in a poem. The act of rehearsing it had become automatic. Now, I try to recognize and consciously choose to instead practice positive mantras.

My go-to "Dave Mantras:"

"Yesterday I was clever, so I wanted to change the world. Today I am wise, so I am changing myself." That's Rumi — a spiritual master from the thirteenth century who kicks me in the ass when I need it the most. Mantras like this one, help me to say goodbye to buying Dave groceries, figuring out his unpaid medical bills, answering his late-night phone calls while listening to nonsensical screaming. My mantras have empowered me to believe that I am not my thoughts. I am the woman who hears those thoughts and can change them. All of them. And the feelings, beliefs, and actions that those thoughts will lead to.

However, when it is especially hard to slow down, reflect, and rethink it, I call a truce. I repeat a mantra in my head to bring peace and love to myself, to Dave, and to the world. "I love you, Dave, my only brother, with a depth and strength that only I can know. I hope to see you soon, brother. Forgive me, for any harm I have caused you, by not working my shit out. If we don't meet up until the gates of Heaven, I hope you're the

Bouncer with a twinkle in your eye and laughter in your heart. I'm so looking forward to kicking your butt again on the basketball court in Heaven, with Tony's cigar smoke swirling around us, just like old times. I love you, my brother, my twin, to the moon and back, just like always."

A FINAL NOTE TO MYSELF ON ADDICTION

"Triggering" is no small thing. If this replay has triggered thoughts and feelings, you've got people. Nar-Anon works. The steps work. They are steps – like Machu Picchu steps but you can climb them. Some days your steps are slow, or you may rest a long time before going up. Some days it feels like you are flying up those steps. Here's a Nar-Anon thought for the day," I will deal with my mistakes and achievements daily. I will make amends immediately, where necessary, and enjoy my accomplishments. In this way, I will maintain my peace and serenity." And in the spirit of Rumi who hinted at it a long time ago but Nar-Anon says it plainly, "We will learn to release the addict and grasp our own recovery... We can only change ourselves."

"Recovery" is going to be life-long. Recovery is going to be different for you than for the rest of your family. Please, please, be mindful when you are climbing those steps that you don't regard where the rest of the family may be on the staircase. They will climb, too, but it's not a race. It's not the time or place for you to throw any of them on your back – you've got enough weight already. We all have our steps to climb, at our own pace, and in our own time.

Remember Teresa – "unconditional love" is what you feel for Dave. For the first fifteen years of your life, you shared almost every important moment with him. You know, truly know, who he is at his center and love him unconditionally because of it. That boy who made you laugh until you peed your pants in aisle four at the grocery store. That boy who missed just about everything the teacher was saying for years, because he couldn't hear, but faked it to fit in. That boy who told you to put on "real" hockey skates, because you could play hockey no matter what the other boys said. That boy who took you aside freshman year of high school and said, "Don't trust a single thing any guy says to you." That young man who wrote a speech senior year on his Kairos retreat, titled "King of Pain." You know him at his center, his true self. Keep his authentic self, close in your heart.

And let the rest go.

TWINS

Grayslake, Illinois 1990
Dave and I in my cousin's wedding, age 21.

II

CHOICE

Partner • Sex • Babies

The act of writing about my early adulthood created a deep sense of gratitude for "choice." I realize that I am privileged. I have been able to choose who I could love, when I could have children, and how I could work in the world. Having a choice in my future has been the most incredible gift. Poems written and rewritten from my early adulthood have allowed me to ask and answer an important question about choice: What kind of person do I choose to be in each moment of each day? The act of writing and rewriting the answer was the next step in my transformation. This was a hard question to answer truthfully but answer I must if I am to fly.

•

PARTNER

•

TRAVELING

For the map makers and treasure hunters

He's the love of my life
we are on this journey together.
But he forgot to bring a map.
He is also not crazy about asking for directions.

I brought him a map — my map of course,
with my routes picked out,
along with final destinations.
Take Pine Street down to the University.
Take the 101 to Burbank for your job in Hollywood.
Take the Alcan Highway straight north to the Kenai River.

He followed the map so well.
Until he didn't.
He laid out his map —
take my name, have my baby,
stay home, take care of our life.

Yikes, now I'm lost.
Those destinations were not on my map.
My map has treasure, at the spot marked "x."
His map had rings, diapers, checkbooks,
and playdates scheduled under a coffee stain.

Take care,
of our journey
that it never ends.

NEGOTIATING THE ROAD OF PARTNERSHIP

I never considered marriage. I considered living in my own apartment, with a dog, in the city, taking the express bus to a civil rights law firm. But marriage, nope. Not for me. Never once did I play "bride" when I was little. Never once did I think about "weddings, proposals, getting down on one knee." It's not that I repelled those notions – they just didn't get any airtime in my imagination. Those dresses looked stiff and heavy, and one certainly could not throw a ball in that get-up.

Then one summer, I went to Alaska for a few months with my best friend, who happened to be my boyfriend. We had no money, no job, and no support for a crazy idea we came up with over a pitcher of beer: road trip to Alaska, 1993. After driving ten thousand miles without tunes, spending three months in a tent, and having the best time being free together, "it" was settled under fireworks on a glacier. And then "negotiating life with another person" began, in earnest. The reality of "marriage" settled in and not just the reality of paperwork, shared accounts, monogamy, babies, or holidays with two families. Marriage changed something fundamental about me and him. And that's when shit got real, the Alaskan honeymoon was over. I would say things like, "Can you PLEASE help me here…..Really? Are you really going out, NOW?... But I think you should…"

I was making the decisions. I was belittling his ability to help with the kids. I was assuming our family was all he needed. I manipulated to get my way. I was making decisions every day that would have giant ramifications for our love and life. Who was I, if not the all-powerful woman who could handle it all? Make all the decisions? "I can work three nursing jobs, get the boys off to school on time, and still have a meal of sorts ready for everyone before I need to be at my next gig." I had to come to some terms with these thoughts, beliefs, and feelings. This next poem captures the anger and righteousness I felt during tough financial times in our marriage. But it also allowed me to pick apart and write about the story of money and power in a relationship.

ROBBING PETER TO PAY PAUL

For my sisters who rob, to feed.

No other way to make it, this month.
No room on the credit cards.
No peanut butter in the cupboard.
Guess I gotta rob Peter, to pay Paul.
She thinks, "how did Peter get so rich,
that he got robbed?"
Now there's the story
they didn't highlight in Sunday school.
Peter got his, from his old lady.
Yes Ma'am, from his old lady.

She was so proud of making her twenty-one an hour.
She was proud of those certificates hangin'
on her bedroom wall.
Still not enough. Not enough to feed her babies.
She stretches the small bit of fish, like her Jesus.
She shops at three church pantries,
but hell, the congregation can talk.
She feeds the chickens and grows her collards,
out back, for her babies.

Don't ask why Peter stole from his old lady.
Don't ask why she just kept it movin'.
It's a story older than the bible.
But next time your money comes up short and you think,
damn, I'm gonna have to rob Peter to pay Paul.
Remember where Peter got his money, honey.

Take Care,
of the old lady gettin' robbed,
barely makin' it.

I had to reckon with the idea that I was pissed off every day for "having to do it all" — passive-aggressive as hell and chest puffed out with righteousness. It didn't occur to me that these thoughts, beliefs, and subsequent feelings were "in my head." These were constructs I adopted that didn't reflect the reality of the situation. We were both working our asses off back then, trying to survive the financial crash of 2008. But I turned my frustration on the person closest to me. I'll never forget the look on my husband's face one night when I became nasty about him not helping with the bills or the kids or whatever. He was on the verge of crying and said in the quietest voice: "I'm not you. I'm trying to figure out who I am. I don't think you want me." That night has rattled me for a long time. I thought and thought and thought about what in the hell did he mean? What was really going on here? The next poem is what I've come up with to capture the love I have always felt for my partner and how I regard him as a man, provider, lover, and father. What it doesn't offer is an explanation for how I can feel deep love, yet still, be so caught up in my head that I'm not fully looking and seeing him. I'm still working on that poem. It's called "I See You."

REGARDING YOUR PURPOSE

For W.B.

I regard your purpose,
your purpose of thought and deed,
much like an admirer wishes
to ride away with you, on your steed.

It is within that moment of the ax
held high above your crown.
As you pause, the air still,
just before bringing it down.

Crack, the wood splits into two neat pieces
of fuel for the fire.
Bringing yourself and spirit, into the coals,
the sparks, the pyre.

That I know you have become the man,
 the wood maker, the provider.
Of Heroes doing right for their babes
nestled within the confider.

Lost in her milk of honey and sweetness
you have been gifted.
From the heavens and goddesses,
watching, as you lifted.

Your ax. Your soul. Your mind.

Your heart. Your being. Even higher.

Taking Care of the babes

at your fire, oh lovely provider.

WHIT AND I

Homer Spit, Alaska 1993
The middle of the night outside our tent just laughing our butts
off after a few Alaskan Ambers, a few days before Whit
popped the question.

•

SEX

•

UNWIND WITH A WHISKEY

For every woman over 50

The mood is slow, low-down, and blue

Ask Miss Bonnie Raitt inside, for a few

Turn up the volume and move on cue

Let her take you to the slow, low-down, and blue.

Love me Like a Man, she beckons you.

Now your shoulders are swaying to and fro

Miss Etta James will keep the groove, the move, the flow

Like a WOMAN she'll tell your soul.

Push all those thoughts of the day outta the way

Enjoy your mood, it's slow, low-down, blues.

Finish it with a bit of righteous doowap with

Miss Lauryn Hill.

She'll make sure you know who's in charge as she fills

You up with her stories of life with the girls

And the slow, low-down, blues.

Take Care of your self-love, ladies.

SEX AND SEXUALITY

Someday you might find yourself naked with the same person for thirty years, saying, "I guess I'll have the bologna sandwich.... again." Nah, it's not that bad. Until it is. What happens to the sex in a relationship as it ages? The change is different for everyone, but change it does. Just the fact that it can and does shift, hurt my self-confidence, my swag. The first time this happened in my late thirties, I did what any young woman would do – I hit the gym and I hit hard like the firefighter I was married to. I got the swing back in my step that picked the sex life back up again. Whew. And just when I got cocky again like all was well in the bedroom department, our late forties snuck up with midlife and financial crises. And with this, the slide back into unforeseen and unwelcome changes in the bedroom. This time, it was different. No quick fix at the gym.

We weren't happy – and I was pissed underneath it all. Pissed as hell, which is woman-speak for scared as shit. Was I just another bologna sandwich? Was I going to become a mid-life crisis trade-in? How come hitting the gym wasn't peeling off those pounds and putting a swag in my swing? Toss in perimenopausal hormones and POOF – the whole thing blows up, right in your face. How many times did I cry after we went out to dinner asking, "Do you even 'want' me?" How many times did he look confused, afraid of the changes in our bedroom, and above all, out of his comfort zone with my insecurities? This next poem is an ode to the insecurities I grapple with as I age, and redefine my sense of self.

'TOX, TITTIES, AND TEETH

For our younger selves

Oh, what a woman will do.

Will do, to hold tight to her younger self.

Her younger self.

She'll inject it, pump it, even replace it,

The telltale signs.

The telltale signs

of mileage, experience, loves lost.

Oh, what a woman will do.

Will do, to hold tight to her younger self.

Is there a possibility that her younger self,

needs to be, set free.

Set free, to fly in the wind.

Taking flight from this world of men.

So that her wiser self may move in.

Move-in, to care for herself.

Care for herself.

In a way that only a wise woman can.

                              Take Care,

        of our younger selves, so we may set them free.

Holding this poem close, I looked around for answers on sex and aging. If you've never read any books on sex and menopause by Dr. C. Northrup or watched an inspirational video by Mama Gena, you haven't seen the other side of what "fifty-plus" can look like. These lovely ladies suggested, strongly, that girlfriend you can still own it. They stressed that who and what I am at this stage in my life is different, but damn, it's still hot. How to regain my confidence took time. Time to find the right combination of support and understanding how I felt about myself. I'm still working on becoming a confident woman who looks deep inside herself and relishes in what she offers the world. I see that my teeth are crooked, my butt is super-sized, and my legs aren't shaved again today, but I now believe I can still bring it. This next "mantra" of sorts that I put together really helped me uncover, "What is passion over fifty?"

HOT AND COOL

For women owning their desires

What does a woman desire,

Asks the Sage of the Mountain.

The Mountain rumbles with laughter

Spilling forth its red hot, hot lava,

Oozing into the unknown.

What does a woman desire,

Asks the Sage of the Ocean.

The Ocean cries out as it crashes with cold, cold water

Pushing in all around its frigid salty waves,

Spinning inside out.

What does a woman desire,

Asks the Sage of the Woman.

To be both Hot and Cool

In every possible way

Says the Woman knowing

Her power in the answer.

Take Care,

Of the dial set too hot, too cool.

Once I wrote this poem, I started wondering what it would take to change the thermometer for me – I needed to find a new temperature. A friend suggested shopping. I'm not a retail therapy kind of gal, but I started there. When the clothes started being delivered, I had an idea. Can the clothes, themselves, change the dial? I put on something other than sweatpants even though we were amid the COVID-19 lockdown at home. What I found was I was changing so much inside myself that the outside no longer expressed who I was becoming. I had no idea how to express my ever-changing self. I heeded excellent advice and consulted with an expert. I found a "stylist" who laughed, listened, and deeply understood how my self-expression was "Under Construction." And, man, did that make all the difference. A professional that can translate "Under Construction" into looking great and feeling great. Crazy. But these women exist! And they are not a fortune – they save you more money on the clothes than it costs to hire them. As Coco Chanel once said, "Elegance is not the prerogative of those who have just escaped from adolescence, but of those who have already taken possession of their future."

My family doesn't even blink anymore as I come down for a Zoom meeting with a dress on and converse high tops. If I'm wearing sweatpants, they still know it's just me, doing my thing. I never would have imagined that I could dress for myself, dress to express myself on each changing day. I'm learning to own my sexuality, embrace my ever-changing body, and most of all, love myself every minute of every day. Writing and rewriting about sexuality and aging has given me the confidence and the "what the hell attitude" to express myself in more ways than one. Here's a recent poem paying homage to the changes I am becoming comfortable with, as my body ages.

Rubbing the Buddha

*For every woman who has rubbed her belly and thought,
"damn girl"*

36-24-36. My measurements at 18.

I don't do sit-ups, and I eat three meals a day.

Magical body casts a spell on unsuspecting passers-by.

No effort required, not one single sit-up.

I slap my belly like Coach slaps the ball.

Knowing it's going to win the game.

42-36-36. My measurements at age 31.

I can't do sit-ups, and I eat five meals a day.

A magical body creates a new life all on its own.

Mythical to all, as it brings forth a soul.

I rub my belly like the devout rub their Buddha.

Knowing it's going to change my world.

36-32-38. My measurements at 52.

I hate sit-ups, and I eat one meal a day.

Magical body craving the cycles of the moon.

I feel my belly resting against my arm, my mattress.

Knowing we're old friends, enjoying the softness.

I rub my Buddha belly, in bliss, with gentleness.

Take Care,

of your Buddha, your comfort, your companion.

CHOICE

A FINAL NOTE TO MYSELF ON KEEPING THE HEAT TURNED UP IN THE BEDROOM

A doctor who thinks losing a few pounds is doable while in menopause and thinks those pounds will be the cure for a low sex drive is full of shit. Fire their ass and get yourself a doctor who understands menopause. Don't make that mistake again.

Remember, to be sexy, you've got to believe it. To believe it, you've got to feel it. To feel it, you've got to think it. So, start with your thoughts, make a plan, execute it, and watch the good times roll. Only you can rediscover your body as it rapidly changes these days. Once you know her, you can love her in the way she needs you to. Maybe that's hormone creams, maybe that's a new dress, maybe that's the keto diet. But only you can find what she needs to think she's hot, believe she's hot, and act hot. It's not about the pounds of time. It's all about the pounds of self-love.

CELEBRATING TWENTY-FIVE YEARS

San Diego, California 2020
Whit and I with our sexy on – even after all these years of marriage.

•

BABIES

•

SELFLESS SEAMSTRESS

For every woman who's held it together
with poor quality thread

We heard the call, to sew the quilt.

A quilt to build the marriage.

We heard the call, to sew a flag.

A flag to lead men into battle.

We heard the call, to sew many masks.

A mask to protect us from the virus.

Threads laid bare around us,

pricked fingers bleeding with our efforts,

comforting sound of strength,

the Singer hums.

We women will mend.

We women will sew.

We women will quilt.

We women will build.

The heart and soul of our family,

our town, our country, and our world.

Take care,

of the selfless seamstress in arms.

74 • TERESA MARTIN

MY BABIES BIRTHED ME

Oh Goddess, I never thought to have babies of my own. They were a foreign lot. The afternoon Whit asked me to have a baby, I was shocked. He just sat on our bed, looked me in the eye, and said, "How about we have a baby?" No warm-up, no preliminary "Let's get a dog." Just, "How about we have a baby?"

Two little boys came into our lives in the next four years. Little rascals really. Full of spizz. All boy. My boys are almost adults now. I don't understand why people use the expression, "it goes by fast." I can tell you that it does not go by fast. I was there each and every day — totally overwhelmed most days, wondering if my husband would ever get home to relieve me for just five minutes of peace. We did the same thing over and over — "Read to me... Help me...Look, Mom!" Over and Over. Time was something else entirely. Nothing went "fast." Writing about that time in my life now, I recognize something I may have missed about those slow-motion moments when the boys were little. Those little moments, when time never went forward, were magic.

There was nothing other than the "now." It was just me and the kids, being in the moment. Doing our thing. Eckhart Tolle once said, "The more you are focused on time — past and future — the more you miss the Now, the most precious thing there is." I wrote the next mantra long ago while breastfeeding my boys. I found it hard to just "sit" and let them breastfeed. My mind wanted to create a "to-do" list, get the laundry done, put some food in my mouth. My prenatal yoga instructor helped me with this mantra, way back then.

Teresa, (exhale)

I am "still,"

I am "here,"

I am "Now."

During this time of complete immersion in an alternate time, called motherhood, I witnessed "transformation." My older son, Roddy, fell in love with a cape during dress-up at school.

He demanded we sew one at home. When he put on his long, blue cape, speckled with bright stars, and a matching hat, he became someone different.   His transformation began. He started telling stories. He made fairy houses for his characters. He talked nonstop about the world he was creating where all the boy-fairies could eat as much candy as they wanted, never go to bed, and drive their bikes recklessly down mountains. His mind opened to new possibilities.   Just the thought of his fairy world made him happy. Happier than I ever saw him. His thoughts drove his emotions.

I could have written this off as "child-like," a "one-off," or "imagination." Until my younger son, Little Whitney, asked for a very different kind of cape. He wanted it green, with leaves, so he could forever live in the forest amongst the flowers and animals. With his cape on, he started bringing roosters up to the house, calmly holding them and talking to them like friends. In case you don't know, roosters don't do "holding by little boys." But his cape transformed him. He was the boy who lived in the forest where no animal was afraid. His body tuned into that frequency and the roosters were now on my front porch, on his lap, swinging in a rocking-chair. Not a cluck, or cock-a-doodle-do, to be heard. It's as if the Buddha was sitting on our porch reminding me, "With our mind, we create our World."

When the poem, "Selfless Seamstress" came out, I had no idea why it was on the page. Over time, the poem showed me that I could be flexible and still strong as I met challenges in my life. The poem allowed me to daydream, remember, and think about sewing capes for the boys when they were little. And I thought, damn, I need a cape. A cape that gives me a sense of peace and happiness – one that changes my very body language and expectations of the world. A cape that brings me unbridled joy.

I began to "sew" my thoughts every day. I weave positive, heart-forward sentiments into my mind, my thinking, my words. I, too, can change my feelings, my energy level, my body language, by thinking differently. "I live in a world where I can write poetry. I can write anything I want. In any way that I want. For any purpose that serves me. There are 'rules', but I can choose to bend them."

BABIES, TO BOYS, TO MEN

I was torn on how to write about my boys now that they are turning into men. I deleted the first, second, fiftieth drafts. Each draft seemed to cross a line that I could not cross any more. Roderick and Whitney, as they prefer to be called now, are almost grown men. It wouldn't be fair to talk about them like I'm still in charge, at the center of their universe, or actually have any "say so" in it anyway. What I do want to say, however, is that it's hard. Real hard. It is hard to step back, watch them take flight and know that they will sometimes fly, sometimes falter, and sometimes fall. On my watch.

I want to hold them up, keep them close, protect them from the strong winds out there. Becoming a mom has been one of the most defining milestones in my life. It has also been the most consistent feedback loop on how I'm doing as a human being. My thoughts, emotions, and beliefs are hardest to take apart and examine when it comes to my boys at this age. Parents of teens and young adults say it over and over but I still wasn't prepared for the: I'm out of control pissed about something they've done, or I'm worried sick about where they are late at night, or I can read the crystal ball of the future that shows a shitty result from a decision they are making. Parenting this age group holds many opportunities for me to exercise positive communication, rethink my beliefs, and take responsibility for my emotions. But I'm a work in progress – and yes, I'm still working on it. And let me tell you, it's taken a good shrink, much patience from my partner, and resilient kids, to put up with my "mom under construction" sign.

In an ode to our relationship of long ago, but honoring the beautiful men they are becoming, I wrote these next two poems. Both are about recognizing how entwined we were when they were little and how the unwinding part has been slow and natural, but as we near their full independence from the nest, it is a sad farewell to our past relationship. I am blessed beyond measure to have brought two beautiful souls into the world and to watch them become soulful men of the future.

A PINCH OF SALT

For Roddy

Beating eggs, watching the yolks swirl round and round.
Soft butter underneath the wax, pinchable, squeezable.
Sugar pouring smoothly from cup to bowl,
the promise of sweetness.

Little pointer finger, brown and ruddy
sneaks into the batter,
catching just a fingertip full of batter.
Licked it up in a split second
with giggles and a twinkle of the eye.

Knowing mother's scolding expression is only
half intended,
she gives him a tasting spoon,
a chocolate bit, declaring
"quality control is an absolute must"
in this kitchen, kitchen of sweetness.

Many years later, he presents her
with a tasting spoon and states quietly,
but with still that twinkle in his eye,
"quality control is an absolute must".

Cinnamon soothes her into remembering,
remembering the recipe of life and love
is right where she left it,
in a pinch of salt.

Take Care,
of my Baker, may you always twinkle.

BUDDHA BABY

For Little Whitney

We spent the morning of your birth alone,
together, smiling at what was to be,
as the birds started to sing.
You came quietly, quickly, and never wanted to leave
from under our cocoon of warmth and honey.

Our first stop on your fifteenth birthday
the giant Buddha, meditating in China Town.
We prayed. We giggled at the size of him.
Magical Day filled with warmth and honey.

Your first take-off by yourself.
You are ethereal when you fly
shoulders too big for the small cockpit.
The plane taking you home,
to your otherworldly self.

When you land back on earth with us, you need more
than you are saying. Rest, here, while your wing repairs.
Tell me what you need. It will be hard,
if it's space. But. You are, ethereal.

Take care,
of my Buddha Baby,
filled with warmth and honey.

A FINAL NOTE TO MYSELF ON MY
BABIES, TIME, AND MAGIC

My boys and our journey together, have made me who I am.
Life truly started for me. My boys birthed me too. They birthed
my sense of "time," my sense of "now," and above all, my sense
of confidence as a woman and a mother.

Teresa — remember transformation happens on the inside, but if
you need help changing something, don't be afraid to ask for
help. You may need to sew a cape, find a therapist, go to a
NarAnon meeting, join a tribe of like-minded people, or call a
friend. Change happens inside us in rich, beautiful, creative ways
when we call upon the magic in the world.

CAPES

Santa Fe, New Mexico 2007
Little Whitney and Roddy, in their hand-made capes and hats,
ready for magic.

III

WOMEN

Safety • Soul Sister • Survivor

My awakening to being a "woman" was both abrupt and a slow burn. As a woman, transwoman, or if you identify as a woman, your "essence" may be the single most amazing part (literally) of your person, or it may be something you fear for. Or a bit of both. My "Women" poems have enabled me to reconcile the complexity of identifying as a woman and how society has influenced my sense of self, confidence, and value.

SAFETY

THE HILL

For my sorority sister, soul sister, and sage

She is at the bottom of the Hill
about to walk up sixty-three
stairs, to her new home at University,
learning to heal is her goal.

She is stopped
with a grab, a pull, a slam, into the wood.
She is overcome with fear, loathing, violation.
It only took a minute, to change her world
at the bottom of the Hill.

She climbs up
to the top of the Hill
every day.
Knowing she will make it,
her legs well-worn, from the climb.

She climbs out of the fear,

the loathing, the violation.

She heals with her faith,

strength, and pride,

her legs well-worn, from the climb.

Take Care,

of our sisters who climb out of violence,

reaching for an education

every minute, every day.

I DREAM OF A WORLD WHERE WE ARE ALL SAFE

From the time I was seven, men frankly scared the shit out of me. An older boy tried to grab my crotch once. And then a basketball coach put his hand on my bare leg when no one was around. My brother's friend told me to take off my shirt, or else he'd tell my brother I had sex with him. My boyfriend in high school smashed my windshield when I broke up with him. I have never spoken of these fears. And real fears they were. I defined these not as "fears" but as "men." I knew "a few good men." But they were not at the forefront of my mind — almost like a dream of what could be, "if only." They did not sway my definition of a man. Even a priest could not sway my definition of "man."

In eighth grade, I went on an informal field trip with our priest and several other girls. I had not, at the time, thought anything strange about our priest until that trip on the boat. Something made the hairs stand up on my neck. I wasn't comfortable enough to say anything to the other girls about the unexpected anxiety I was feeling. Something was not right. I wish with all my heart I had shared this with the other girls, with my grandmother, with anyone. But I didn't. No one else seemed to sense the fear. Just me. I stopped volunteering to read scripture at Mass. I stopped going to the family nights the Priest held for kids of divorced parents. I stopped accepting invites out with the girls on his boat. I tucked this away. Twenty years later, I saw our Priest's name in the Chicago Tribune — he was one of thirty-two accused in the sex scandal of the century. Two middle school girls had accused him of sexual assault only two years before he arrived at our Parish, but he was never convicted. The guilt I have for not saying anything plagues me. My faith in religion ran dry. I pray that nothing happened to any of the other girls. I pray that the girls who did come forward are healing. I may not have religion, but I pray. What else can a woman do? Where's the blueprint for this? I can't believe there's no blueprint.

But then I found a blueprint in the strangest place – a Buddhist Nunnery. There, at the base of Mount Everest, lives close to 400 women and girls who wear orange-burgundy capes. This community of women live, work, and pray to create a world where they can live safely in Kathmandu – in their community with an alarming presence of sex traders, their community with staggering poverty, their community seeped in patriarchal dogma, their community of the legendary "man against mountain" mystique at the base of Everest.

They call themselves the Kung Fu Nuns. They came up with a blueprint for standing in their own power. They make it look easy – easy to do, free to implement, culturally relevant, and at its core, radical. Radical enough for any American hardline feminist to appreciate its' elegant design to protect, empower, and enrich the lives of girls and women. And they do it to the backbeat of Beyonce singing "Run the World (Girls)." They post mantras that are recited in the monastery. My favorite, "A strong woman looks a challenge in the eye and gives it a wink."

They teach Kung Fu so young girls aren't captured by sex traders. They teach every girl how to work in technology, agriculture, and health education. All trades that are desperately needed in their community. They teach the balance of kung fu and prayer – knowing when to fight and when to pray, to keep women and their communities safe. I will come to understand their playbook and replicate what wins. For girls everywhere. My intuition tells me these are my people and I need to share their story. Here's the poem they've inspired – it has inspired another book. I can't wait to start writing about their blueprint and share it with the world.

THE KUNG FU NUNS

For the warrior in all of us, who wields her mighty sword

I wanted to be a Nun when I was young, walked away
because their smiles came only, with righteousness.
Then I found a new Nun.
A Nun who trains three hours a day,
who wields a sword, who quotes Beyonce,
who winks with a glint in her eye.

A Nun who travels
thousands of miles through the Himalayas
to find girls – girls who are sold,
sold unknowingly, into a life of slavery.
Girls who may become no one, to anyone.
Until she was someone to a Nun.

A Nun who enters into cities that no NGO will go to,
to rebuild – rebuild with her bare hands,
one brick at a time. All sweat.
All smiles. All training.
All praying. All saving.

Take care,
I'm coming, with my mighty sword.

A FINAL NOTE TO MYSELF ON SAFETY

This picture is why you had to talk about being "safe." Remember her, hold her hand, lead her forward. She needs you. Others like her need you. Now and always. As the Dalai Lama and Desmond Tutu have reminded you, "Courage is not the absence of fear but the triumph over it."

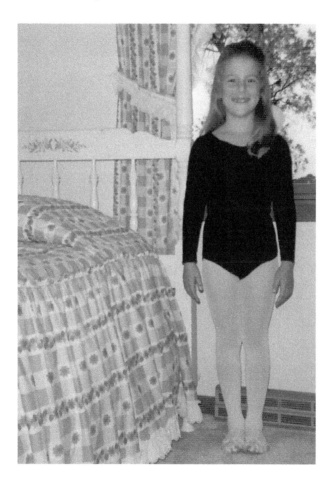

GYMNAST, BALLPLAYER, GIRL

Grayslake, Illinois 1970s
Me wearing my first leotard ready for gymnastics class.

•

SOUL SISTER

•

PREGNANT FRIENDS

For my soul sisters who have been to the crossroads

The third trip to "the clinic" was the hardest.

The receptionist mistook me for the patient.

My dear sweet friend was at her crossroads.

She wasn't ready to be a mother.

Hands shaking. Chest heaving.

Hair unwashed, smelling old,

like she had seen much life, in a short time.

Put on this gown, read this, watch the video,

alone. No visitors allowed.

No Doctor to tell her what she really needed to know

she had a friend, waiting without judgment.

She was a good person, her Goddess loved her.

It was ok to cry, letting out the depth of sadness.

It was ok to grieve for the spirit inside her,

she would never be the same either way.

She, like the others, never talked about that day again.

We went to bars, studied in libraries,

watched football games,

dated and loved new partners.

But I saw her pain sometimes, fleeting, underneath.

She knew I knew. She would blink away a tear,

give a small, pained look of acknowledgment.

Take care,

of my blessed friends

mothers to the unborn.

Friendship and Support

When I wrote this poem about taking more than one friend to an abortion clinic in college, I was surprised by it. I had not thought of those exact moments for many, many years. It was a poem that opened up a different side of myself. I support other women in their greatest hour of need without judgment. I understand that I could never know why or how a person makes decisions, but I still have deep empathy and love for them. I was raised Catholic-light, which is very Catholic-heavy on the issue of life and death. I am proud of myself for being able to openly, genuinely, and completely love and support another woman, no matter what I may have been "taught," how others may "think," or what institutions may "prescribe." Friendship isn't about having the same views, politics, or pastimes. It's about love and support. No matter what. This was the first poem I wrote that allowed me to see my strengths. It was a powerful moment to hold.

Friendship and Honesty

Here's my truth on friendship. Sometimes, I don't want to hear the truth. Sometimes, I don't understand where in the hell you are coming from. And sometimes, I just want to stop talking. Maybe it's weird for a woman to hold these ideas, but that's my truth. Here's an example. I told myself that I needed to lose twenty pounds. I did it. I visited "Friend" and gave her my good news. Even showed her how good I looked in those new jeans. She agreed with me. She said "Yes, you needed to lose the twenty pounds. I can't imagine you weighing that much to begin with" My response in my head: "Who in the hell is she, to tell me I needed to lose twenty pounds? Bitch, have you checked out your ass lately?"

I was hoping for an "atta girl you look great," but instead I got "yes, you needed to lose twenty pounds." She's being honest — just like all the good stories about friendship have instructed her. I wasn't looking for honesty, I was looking for validation, confidence, maybe even a little bullshit like

"You didn't need to lose that much, my God, have another cookie." I knew this needed a poem. It took a long time to get something out that was honest about empathy, emotional exchange, and friendship. I turned to the Dalai Lama and chose meditation many, many times to guide me, "As you breathe in, cherish yourself. As you breathe out, cherish all beings."

I HAVE A CONFESSION

For the listener, the speaker, and the place in between

A little confession I have to share,

if you'll hear. It's just a wee bit of truth,

niggling at my soul, I fear.

A truth as old as time, but hard to feel,

just the same. I didn't understand the pain of others,

yes, it is a shame. I didn't feel the true emotional weight

behind their words. It escaped me, just out of reach.

I think it may be too late,

to help them back, from their hate.

All I am left with is this confession,

of a person paid to hear

of all the pains and sorrows of another's fears.

But knowing she doesn't really quite begin to feel.

Take Care,
of my feelings, yet they come too late.

Writing this poem was like getting hit over the head. Friendships, their dialogue, their ups and downs, their pitfalls and their triumphs are not truly about the other person. Are they about me? Am I able to really feel empathy for my friends? Am I able to love myself? Excellent questions that I immediately wanted to say "YES" to but knew that I needed to gradually start the journey to truth. The truth of how I feel about myself, the truth of how I *want* to feel about myself, may just be the single most important indicator of my capacity to be in friendship.

A FINAL NOTE TO MYSELF ON FRIENDSHIP

The "mirror exercise" has been the single most powerful exercise for me to get to my truth. My truth about feeling good about and loving myself right here, right now. And when I love myself in truth, I really am a great friend. A great friend to myself and others.

When you meet your "soul sisters," you know who they are pretty quickly. They are the women who bring your best self forward. Your person who is filled with empathy, compassion, light, love, and joy. I am grateful every day for having many friends who I can call my soul sisters.

Oh, and by the way, remember Teresa — the friend in the picture would never tell you that you need to lose twenty pounds. She'd just buy you both another bag of Oreos and make it movie night. But she is the Gal that has never had any trouble looking herself in the mirror and saying "I love you." She's my soul sister, my hero.

GROWING UP TOGETHER

Hollywood, Florida 1978
Sheila and I as young girls on roller skates (how 70s).

•

SURVIVOR

•

RISE

For my sisters learning to FLY

RISE — get up

FIND — your stance

LOOK — it in the eye

SEE — yourself, others

OWN IT — RIGHT NOW

PLAN — to do right by your sisters

DO — decisive action

FINISH — no woman left behind

CELEBRATE YOUR POWER

VIOLENCE HAPPENS. OUR RESPONSE IS CRITICAL.

When I was a senior in high school, I broke up with my boyfriend the day after prom while we sat in my car at the beach. He took his fist and smashed my windshield from the passenger seat. I said nothing, drove him home, and then told my parents what happened to their car. They asked me to ensure that he reimburse them the two hundred dollars to replace the window. That's it. No one called him out on reprehensible behavior. No one told his parents. Nothing. Just a phone call asking for the money. I don't even remember if he paid them. I do remember my family and friends asking me over the next few days, "What could you have possibly said to him, that would have caused such a strong reaction?" My adult self is sarcastically saying with a lot of attitude, "Really? I said something to cause this?" But my seventeen-year-old-self quietly thought, "I'm stupid for breaking up with him the day after prom. He must be really hurt."

I needed someone to be an ally. I needed to be honest with myself that the situation was scary as hell and wrong on every level. I needed someone, anyone, to say that I did nothing wrong. I needed to say it to myself. A woman will blame herself for violence unless she has an ally. Staying quiet, keeps violence alive. I was recently with the strongest woman I know, but after a long night filled with many glasses of wine, she told me a story of surviving repeated violence in her previous marriage that shook me to my knees. I could not believe that I didn't know about or suspect it. I could not believe that I froze and didn't know how to respond. I couldn't believe that I was acting like the people around me the day after prom. This is the poem I wrote to her. I was trying to capture her strength as I see her now and acknowledge that I was ill equipped on how to support such a strong woman, but was going to figure it out. No matter what. I was going to embrace the teachings of Desmond Tutu and the Dalai Lama, "Each and every moment, we are able to create and recreate our lives and the very quality of human life on our planet. This is the power we yield."

BROKEN THUMB

For L.J.M.

She stood under the harsh kitchen light,
middle of the night, many glasses of wine.
She rubbed her thumb, massaging a deep hidden spot.
Looking down as she massaged and flexed,
she said, "he broke my thumb, you know."

She was not looking for sympathy.
She was not looking for shock.
She was not looking for a soul.
She was looking inside.
Inside her broken thumb.
Massaging it.

Remembering her strength.
Remembering that she left.
Remembering that she made it out.
Her thumb had healed over the decade.

But there was still a deep hidden spot.
Of remembering.
Where she went to remind herself.
Of her strength.
Of her healing.
Her healing in deep hidden spots.

Take care,
of her healing and remembering.

When I started to explore violence in my life and the life of others through my poetry, the universe sent me a math equation via Jack Canfield. The world is indeed a quirky place. The math equation: E+R=O. E=event, R=response, O=outcome. Violence is an event that happens every day to women. How we recover (our outcome) is dependent on the "response." I am going to use violence as the event since it calls into question, "who's response?" Since women have no control over how others will respond to an accusation of violence, they can only change her own response to violence. After my boyfriend smashed my windshield in high school, my response was to blame myself, not question others' responses, and bury the memory as deeply as possible. I believe that my response was culturally and systematically prescribed. I think the only way women are going to have better outcomes after violent events, is if we teach each other alternative responses. And yes, I am calling to tear down the system here. "MeToo" showed incredible support for women and provided a platform to tell their story. It's time to take it to the next level: "NotMyFault," "ThisSucks," "PutHisAssInJail," "NeverAgain."

A FINAL NOTE TO MYSELF ON VIOLENCE

Teresa – Figure out how you can change the system through your actions, one woman at a time. Show every woman she has an ally so she can speak out against injustice and violence. So she can respond differently. You know where staying quiet has gotten you – nowhere. You may have all the best intentions in the world, a great plan, and even a helluva speech, but if you don't take action, it doesn't mean jack. If you keep your thoughts, feelings, conclusions, ideas, and passions locked up inside yourself, afraid of making the wrong move, no one will benefit from what you have to give. A young woman may never know she has an ally. A strong woman may never know she can lean on you. Teresa – get your ass moving. Take action. Fly, girl, fly.

As Strong As

Santa Fe, New Mexico, 2020
My friend Sabrina, my son Whitney, and Me in full support of
one another during Covid.

IV

CHALLENGES

Career • Money • Loss

We all have "challenges." Through my poetry, I have found that some of my challenges have become my kryptonite. Kryptonite is real. We all have our own special brand of it. Maybe yours is that third glass of wine, that girl-on-the-side of your marriage, those extra thirty pounds of stress, that work-until-you-drop mentality, the negative thoughts plaguing your every turn. My kryptonite was my sense of duty on the job, my negative feelings about money, and the ungrieved losses of people and places I hold dear.

My poems about my kryptonite pushed me to acknowledge that I was embracing ideas and habits that were killing my inner love, peace, and joy. My poems also gave me the tools to neutralize my kryptonite and rise with a strength of positive thinking, joy in my heart, and compassion for the souls around me.

CAREER

SAN FRANCISCO, 1991

For my Fearless Soul Sisters

San Francisco was my first love, and first patient, really.
Free, open, sex, blunts, pawn.

The hospital bed was so big. She was so small,
and black, and quiet, and dry to the touch.

Her six foot, three-hundred-pound mother with a durag
stomped into the room, demanded my name.

My patient, but really my sage,
whispered to her mother, "she's hospice."

All three hundred pounds stared in my direction
and throated, "hmmmf."

I'm hospice? Fuck. I've got no call bell for Jesus.
Just some poorly printed pamphlets on dying.

My first patient's, last words,
"I'm Black, I'm Gay, I'm a Woman, I'm from the South."

"I have AIDS. Who would choose that?
Tell my mama that — tell her I had no choice."

> Take Care,
> Of the Fearless,
> Fighting for her Life,
> Fighting for her Place,
> In this world and the next.

WHY AM I A CAREGIVING MACHINE?

I'm a nurse. And nurses don't lie, cheat, or steal. They breed that out of you in nursing school. They also tap into your basic nature as a caregiver and use it to build you into a caregiving machine. My first "patient," before I even went to nursing school, has been my guiding light for all these years. The poem, "San Francisco, 1991" is an ode to her wisdom. I will never forget her name, what she looked like, how she sounded, or how her skin felt. I will never forget the single most important lesson she taught me. There are things outside of our control, like where and who we were born as. And there are things we have absolute control over, like how we care for one another.

Her wisdom continues to guide me as a caregiver, especially now, as nurses are called to action over and over. Both my grandmothers, one a nurse and one who wanted to be a nurse, showed me that nurses are essential. What I learned on the job is that nurses are caregivers times a thousand. We give and we give. But why? I just can't put my finger on it. Especially in 2020. Two hundred nurse's white shoes were placed on the steps of the White House at the beginning of the COVID-19 pandemic – representing the nurses who died in the line of duty. Six months in, the numbers were estimated over 900. Twelve months in, the numbers are in the thousands worldwide. We're dying on the front line. We don't have adequate supplies to protect us from this fate. A vaccine has come, along with a mutated virus. But how do nurses respond? We volunteer to give care at natural disasters in our "free time," we work extra shifts to relieve some of the burden from other nurses, we quarantine, separated from our families, in order to keep them safe. Our patients, starting with my first patient in San Francisco, are our "everything." We will have the hard conversations, we will hold your dying hand, we will fight for your life.

In this next poem, I talk about a particularly gut wrenching twelve hour shift I pulled as a nursing student. At the end of the poem, I acknowledge that myself and my culture did not have any way to cope with the death of a child so I leaned on the tradition of the Iroquois. I tried to remember an Iroquois chant recorded by Joanne Shenandoah and sing it to my patient while she was passing.

TWELVE HOUR SHIFT

For every woman who has held the dying child

Pediatric Oncology rotation.
One nursing student was delighted, all white-teeth-smile,
God-is-with-her-and-is-guiding-her hyperbole.
She must not be a mother.
Never felt the dropping of her baby in her womb,
the slick delivery relieving the pressure,
the rhythmic tug of letting down her milk.

Orders flashed on screen, change a sterile bandage.
Orders screamed in silence, comfort the dying child.
She crawled into the nurse's arms
strength of a lion she held otherworldly still
through the smell of betadyne.
Bloating of the belly round and hard.

Docs rounded, said nothing, left no hope but
heads shaking, heavy shoulders. No new orders.
She stared into my eyes, her eyes enormous and blue,
with a knowing that I could not know.
She slept in my arms, pressed against the vibrations
of humming rhythms from long ago women.

Twelve hours. A Nurse's time.

Take Care,
of small feet pattering in their heavens,
and the women who deliver them.

This experience moved me in many ways. It returns to me in dreams especially as I consider, "Why in the hell am I a nurse?" It has allowed me to ask myself, "Is nursing my calling or my kryptonite?" I wrote this next poem to explore how I felt about being a nurse in 2020. It was almost easier to focus on just one year instead of the entire career choice. Nurses were hit hard in 2020. Our frustration with our leadership both on the ground and in the White House was palpable. Our dismay at our communities who would not help protect one another by simply wearing a mask kept us up at night. Our death toll, which absolutely could have been reduced, will be the legacy our community, country, and world will have to reckon with. Make no mistake, when this thing is further behind us, nurses are coming. And we're coming in hot. Hot for change. Hot for accountability. And hot for revolution.

WHITE SHOES AT THE WHITE HOUSE

For my community of Nurses

Black and white photo of Nurse Anne staring stoically,

white hat, ironed crisp, pinned over knotted hair,

indicating a seriousness of purpose,

a woman with intention.

Shoulders straight, ramrod.

No hint of the curves underneath,

the white dress stiff with starch,

a bold order in hand, to set

the world right again, on its feet again.

A woman wearing white leather shoes,

no scuffs or muddied edges, well worn.

The white shoes walk with the Doctor.

The white shoes rest

while she holds the dying man's hand.

The white shoes are cleaned of their bloodied story.

The white shoes of the nurse, the nurse who heals,

the nurse who brings light, to the sick and the dying.

Two hundred pairs of White Shoes were placed

on the steps of the white house today.

Removed from the healing sisters and brothers

who will no longer clean their shoes of blood,

rest quietly to hold a dying man's hand,

walk with their tribe of healers, ere again.

Take Care,

of the Healers, bloodied shoes and all.

A FINAL NOTE TO MYSELF ON CAREERS

Teresa — You love helping people. You spent eight months writing and rewriting, "What is my purpose in life." You repeated Rumi's words over and over to find your purpose, "Let yourself be silently drawn by the strange pull of what you really love. It will not lead you astray." Your life's purpose, after all this time, still looks pretty damn close to a description of a nurse and therapist. Don't let the system or situation turn your purpose into your kryptonite. You're still figuring out how to open yourself up to all the possibilities that exist for your own healing and to help others heal. That poem has turned into a for-purpose company. — TeresaMartinINK.

NURSE ANNE

Little Chute, WI 1931
My Grandmother's nursing school graduation picture.

•

MONEY

•

LOOK CLOSELY AT THE OFFER OF MARRIAGE

For the woman engaged to her future

Ring finger, heavy with the weight of a diamond.

"Don't ride the subway,

your fiancé can't afford insurance."

White dress, heavy with the weight of fabric.

"Don't sit down,

your father spent our retirement on fittings."

Guest list heavy with guilt.

Crossed off persons.

"We're not inviting them at two–twenty–five per plate."

Honeymoon heavy with five stars of style.

"He can afford

to take you somewhere better."

Women, engaged to their future,

Leave the money on the table.

Take the boy (or the girl)

who becomes the man (or the woman)

who becomes the beauty

who becomes the love

who becomes the soul

of it all.

Take Care,

of the offer of marriage.

MONEY, MONEY, MONEY

Do you see the power of poetry? I can even say the word
now. "Money." I married for love, not money. Now I ponder,
"Both would have been nice." He'll laugh when he reads this and
thinks, "Damn, I knew she'd catch on at some point." My poem
on money and marriage offered me insight into the complexity
of marriage. I actually refused an engagement ring at the
age of 25, stating that "no man was going to buy me" and we
settled on two simple gold bands, inscribed on the inside with
a message for only us to know. But I can tell you that money
almost destroyed our marriage. Not the fact that we didn't have
any. But our attitude about it. We both drank the cultural Kool-
Aid about money. "Put your nose to the grinder," "work harder,"
"money doesn't grow on trees." This is an attitude of scarcity.
That there is not enough money in the world to go around.

FROM BROKE TO ABUNDANCE

My relationship with money did not get off to a good start in life.
The taste of money was bitter for many years. My response was
to put my head down and work and work and work. Work until
I didn't know what a vacation felt like. There was actually a year
that I worked three nursing jobs. Three. If you're a nurse, you
know what this means. It's damn near impossible. But that's how
I dealt with it. Until my mind just broke. I was technically "off"
for Christmas, but I was on the phone triaging patient calls most
of the night, instead of spending our holiday vacation together.
That was it. The tipping point. I missed lighting the farolitos.
I missed dessert. I missed stuffing the stockings. I missed everything
I held dear on the one night that I took off. I drove home and I
quit my job. Cold turkey.

After that I had time. Time to read books about "abundance."
The books, recommended I create a positive mantra around money,
"I am open to health, wealth, and abundance." Still coming
from a place of scarcity, I figured "Why not? Mantras are free."
The very same day that I recited my first mantra, I found a dollar
bill on the elevator floor. I picked it up and wrapped up inside
of the dollar was a sticky note. I stood in the elevator, in a stupor.

The sticky note said, "Blessings One. Blessings are coming to you... Just believe and keep going. Much abundance is all around you." I thought my husband was playing a joke on me. He was the only one who knew about the reading and how I was pursuing a different mindset about money. When I picked my jaw off the elevator floor and went back to our apartment, I found him innocent.

Here's the ass kicker. One year later, our tax returns were exactly what I asked for from the universe on that day I found the sticky note. Exactly what I had asked for. All the while, I pursued my passions and my purpose. How did I come by income without working full time or three nursing jobs for that matter? The strangest opportunities came into my life that I would normally have blown off. But with my new attitude, I pursued them and they paid off in cold hard cash. Everything from increased royalties from promoting a long-ago published book to learning a little Stock Market Investment 101 to hiring an accountant to recouping overpaid taxes. Things I had never considered in my realm of possibilities, started paying. I just needed to focus on them, figure out "how to," and just "do it." Once I cleared my negative attitude and became open to possibilities, I found them all around me.

There are scores and scores of books out there and not enough space here to give you the 411 on making money doing what you love. Writers are always avid readers, but we're talking a ridiculous number of books here. You name it, I've read it or it's in my lineup. But here's my "bottom-line" takeaway: I needed to change my attitude about money from "I need money to survive" to "I want money to choose." As money continues to stream into my life fluidly and in abundance, I am grateful for the choice it gives me.

A FINAL NOTE TO MYSELF ON MONEY

Teresa — remember that you can do whatever you want with money. You can choose to give it away freely to the Equal Justice Initiative. You can choose to travel to Kathmandu to write a story on the Kung Fu Nuns. You can choose to meditate in Bali. You can choose to surf in Costa Rica. You can choose the ocean view Malibu retreat house to live in. You can choose to start your own "for purpose" company. Choices. Money in abundance brings you choices.

Mantra with me, girl: *choices*. I can choose to use money to pursue my passions and serve the world.

Teresa — Ask for help. You found nonprofits, for profits, accountants, lawyers, and financial advisors who all gave you their time, expertise, and resources freely just because you came to them with a few questions, a humble heart, and your story.

Teresa — Do whatever it takes to believe in the power of money to make choices. It's not power over people. It's the power of choice. And there is more than enough to go around.

MANIFESTING MY BACKYARD IN MALIBU

Burbank, California 2020
Illustrated by Teresa Martin

·

LOSS

·

MY AFFAIRS ARE NOT IN ORDER

For Roddy and Little Whitney

Heaviness. The weight of a wave,
pinning my chest to the bed.
No wheezing or gasping.
Just quiet, shallow breaths.
No one to call for help – husband is working
can't be disturbed at the firehouse.
Children on my bed, whining for something.
Not really sure what they want.
Confused. Hard to stay focused. Find the phone.

Riding to the ER in the neighbor's backseat,
dirt road with deep potholes.
Every bounce shortened the shallow breaths.
Pain piercing my right 5th intercostal.
Unable to ask the neighbor to slow down.
Unable to inhale.

The ER nurse maintains her professional voice
she reads the monitor.
Transparent to another nurse, though.
I manage to whisper "no vents."
Glances all around the triage bay.
Now they recognize me, a nurse.

The MD insinuates that I must have AIDS to be so sick,
from a respiratory illness at thirty-eight.
Not one, but two negative HIV tests.

Where is my family? I'm alone here.
The O2 tank is loud. Lights too bright.
Where are my clothes? No blanket. I'm shaking.
My left arm is cold and swollen. IV looks blown.
Can't hit the call bell. Too tired.

Sticky, wet, blood everywhere.
I have to get up and put in a tampon.
Got to get the kids their snack before naptime.
What day is it? Just let me go home.
My affairs are not in order. My affairs are not in order.

Take Care,
of my love, my boys, my life.

THE SPIRITUALITY OF TRANSITIONING IN LIFE

This first poem is about my own scrape with death. It allowed me to think about how accustomed to death I am at work and how I haven't grieved for the losses I've experienced, both in my life and on the job. Before I could tackle grief, I had to tackle transitions. In the moment right before a baby is born or a person dies, they transition. It's only for a moment or two, but it is the unsaid moment we don't talk about. It's time to talk about it, my poems said.

We transition in and out of ourselves, in and out of the world. Being both a Labor & Delivery and Palliative & Hospice nurse illuminated how transitioning patients into and out of this world is really similar. Souls come into this world quietly, or with much drama, or with complications during the ride. Souls leave this world sometimes quietly in the night, sometimes with much suffering, or sometimes with complications during the journey.

Both entering and leaving the world, are a given in a persons' life. However, we often feel unprepared for both. We come totally unprepared for the emotional and spiritual journey we must take, to bear witness to a soul's transition. I was unprepared the first time I watched someone die. It was an existential experience filled with spirits and otherworldly winds, whipping all around me. I was a very scientific, logical fifteen-year-old with no belief in religion, heaven, the afterworld. I was actively rebelling against my Catholic School education. And then there I was, walking into the room, and my grandfather was taking his last breaths.

I felt spirits all around me, brushing up against me, lifting him. It sounds like a ceiling painting at the Vatican, but I swear it was real. So real, that my grandmother, who was not a strong believer in anything, was looking around the room at the same spirits. We didn't talk about that moment for many years. When we did, we were both so relieved that the other person had "seen" it too. She came to me in a dream after her own death to tell me once again that it was all very real. I wrote this next poem about her death. It took place on my twenty-third birthday. Transitions to and from this world are, indeed, intertwined. After writing this poem, I experienced a sense of healing from the deep grief I have carried since her death. I revealed how mixed up it was in my head – birth, death, desires.

BIRTHDAY WISHES

For birthday wishes left unwished for

Gertie was my mother's mother who didn't know

a mother's mother, could be a mother again.

My mother kept her mother with her until the end.

The end of it all. The end of it all.

My birthday morning, mother phoned me

not with birthday wishes

but death wishes. Death wishes.

Wishes for me to take the next flight home.

Wishes to give the eulogy.

Wishes to find my brother, in some bar on the north side.

Wishes. Wishes. Wishes.

My wish: that my mother's mother

would still be my mother

and send me birthday wishes. Birthday wishes.

Take Care,

of my mother's mother, oh mother of us all.

I was unprepared for my own first scrape with death. It snuck up on me without knowing what in the hell was going on. I never saw it coming, until I saw the nurse's face in the ER. Then I knew. I was a patient who was told to put my affairs in order while my 38-year-old husband with two small children stood by. The gripping fear, confusion, anger, and helplessness is overwhelming when a doctor tells you to put your affairs in order. I remember just barely having the strength to look over at my family and blink back tears. Providence and my young athletic body would not give up on me just yet, though. The first day I was able to hang on to the side rails of the hospital bed and hoist myself upright to standing was a blessed day. That was the day I knew I'd be okay. I'd see my boys grow up. I'd feel the warmth of my husband sleeping next to me again. After a very long year, I got my life back to 100%. A blessing I hold gratitude for every day. A blessing I pray for with each and every one of the patients under my care now, twelve years later, as COVID dominates our work and world.

But what I wouldn't know, until after I slowly recovered, was that I would lose something else that was so dear to me, that I haven't talked about it until now, twelve years later.

We lost our Ranch.

OUR RANCH

For our home, our New Mexico

We buried all our pets
under the Pinon Tree on the hillside
bears gathering in Fall.

We built the tree house,
to scale, from the book, "The Dangerous Book for Boys"
the secret password, "GROSS," ode to Calvin and Hobbes.

We planted and dug, from scratch,
an orchard of dozens of specially grafted heritage apple trees
running the Acequia we cut with shovels and rakes.

We raised a barn, fed chickens named Rocky, Bev, and Silkie
sold their eggs to neighbors,
in hand painted egg cartons.

We tended the soil with compost, worms, and
chicken droppings for years to create a sustainable garden
nourishing us through many months of the year.

We heard Santa stomping on the roof with sleigh bells,
bringing his delights, and almost falling off the roof
one particularly snowy winter.

We showered under a water containment system,
outside behind the kitchen, reusing our water
for the strawberry patch no one thought would bear.

We chopped Pinons, Junipers, and Cedar
wood to feed the stove
keeping us warm all winter.

We ate Elk the boys harvested from the land,
giving thanks for our food, knowing
where it came from and the cost of life.

We pinned both a firefighter and nurse,
embarking on professions that spoke to our hearts,
brought us into our community.

We knew only the ways of the woods, without internet or screens,
building fairy houses, zip lines, and river-crossing tree swings.
Our Ranch where we lived in the rhythm of New Mexico.

HEALING

Writing that poem about our ranch, has led to so much healing. I couldn't look at pictures from our life back then until I wrote and rewrote that poem. I just couldn't. I felt responsible for losing everything my family held dear. My hospital bills and my inability to understand a shady mortgage deal, resulted in foreclosure. We fled New Mexico with hurt so deep in our hearts, it took me twelve years to open the door of my inner world where our ranch was tucked inside. I finally looked at the pictures. I cried. I roadtripped in the middle of the pandemic to go straight to our ranch to "see it." And what I found was the loveliest family working to heal the land after twelve years of neglect since we departed. We walked the acequia. We walked the property line. We walked to every tree, shrub, and vine I had planted.

I am healing by looking at the pictures, feeling the soil in the garden again, and crouching down inside the coop we built. Until I acknowledged that this loss was lethal kryptonite, I couldn't grasp how much of my life had been dulled out. I would not let the sunshine in or grow attachments to anything since we left our ranch. I left every job I had after two years in order to avoid deep connections to any person, place, or kind. I turned inward and left my friendships out in the wind. I allowed my loss, my guilt, to be kryptonite.

A Final Note to Myself on Loss

Teresa – It's never convenient to face loss. It's never convenient to heal. It's never convenient to neutralize your kryptonite. You let twelve years be run by your loss and guilt. Twelve years. That's more than half your boys' lives. There is no way writing a poem could open that door all alone.

Teresa – Your "people" have given you the strength to open that door. You have found community this year in the most unusual places – online groups, writer's groups, self-help groups. With their positive energy, they have given you the strength to feel held in support. To feel and experience deep healing.

You let people in. And they are holding you lovingly in their outstretched arms.

Remember Teresa – the world is filled with magic and wonderful people, if you just let it in.

MY BOYS WAITING FOR ME TO COME HOME FROM THE HOSPITAL

Our Ranch, Chupadero, New Mexico 2008

V

MY PURPOSE

Intentions • Art • People • Process

The power in authoring and reauthoring my thoughts through poetry and prose has been the single greatest tool to move my dial, to transform me. I used writing, drawing, coloring, sculpting, photography, videoing, reciting, sewing, and even surfing to author and reauthor my life this year.

I am transforming my narrative, my life, my present, past, and future, into exactly what I want. Into exactly what I am meant to do with great purpose. Into exactly who and how I want to be in this world.

Here's where I get to watch my inner little girl, smile, run, and fly toward her destiny. My passions will guide me. The ideal world I want to live in, will guide me. The Universe will conspire with me. My grandmother would tell me, "you can do anything, honey. You can fly."

Now step out into the Light, Smiling, and Fly.

FLY GIRL, FLY

For my Readers

CHART — your course

GOODBYE — say it with meaning

OPEN — the door and step out

WALK — with head held high

SMILE — and greet new beginnings

SKIP — in gratitude

BELIEVE — with the Universe

RUN — in pleasure of your own strength

FLY — GIRL, FLY

MY INTENTIONS

I wanted to know more about the internal process of transformation when I read "how to" books. They gave me lovely examples and anecdotes, but I wanted the meat. The real meat – what does the process of really changing your life look and feel like, from the first person perspective. I wrote what I couldn't find. And in the process, I reauthored my life into the life I want to live. I kept this quote near my computer over the last year by Rumi, "Don't be satisfied with stories, how things have gone with others. Unfold your own myth." His words kept me writing.

I wanted to surround myself with like-minded people from all over the world for support, in real ways, from weekly check-ins, to keeping each other accountable for making change, to being a resource for one another with our respective expertise, to sharing a cup of coffee over Zoom with laughter in our hearts. As I entered this community, I found that "self-help" and "self-care" are total misnomers. Community care is where the real change and transformation takes place. I found Alchemists all around me. I love how Paulo Coelho describes the alchemist, "That's what alchemists do. They show that, when we strive to become better than we are, everything around us becomes better, too."

My intentions from the start were always so clear to me: tell my story in the first person so that someone else will have the "meat" of what transformation may look like and, share my transforming self with others so that we may together create the world into a community that deeply cares for one another.

•

MY ART

•

It took me a long time to own my thoughts. Now that I own them, it is time to share. Not all my thoughts, but the ones that are still important to me and may be important to you. What age has provided is the truth that my experiences in life are unique to me and universal to womankind.

Experience gives me permission to speak from my place of truth. Knowing that it is only MY place of truth – not shared. All the while still knowing that my truth and the stories they hold are just as important as the next person's. There is no real truth, just our own. My stories and poems may hit close to the bone for some, be wildly out of the comfort zone for others, and raise questions about my beliefs and hopefully yours too.

Writing poems to capture the essence of what I have to say while pairing an essay for context has been an evolving process, quite like aging. Start with the bare bones and go deeper, get more real, keep seeking what drives me and own it. All of it. When I'm scared to put my "treasonous" thoughts on paper, I reread J. Olson, "Turning words into art is unnatural... It says I am unhappy with the way things are and desire to make things different... I will make something wildly and savagely new... It disrupts and shatters... Dangerous feelings vented from a cage of skin... It goes to the heart of creativity."

•

MY PEOPLE

•

I've asked five women to join me in this section to talk about the creative collaboration we have developed over the last six to twelve months while working on this book. Each of these women has given me the gift of themselves. They have cared for me in ways that I did not know was even possible. They have gifts of immeasurable strength and insight that I know they will share with the world exponentially. I've asked them to tell a little bit about our journey and why they went along for the ride. I've also encouraged them to offer themselves to you as well. They have given you a place to find them and share in their gifts. Each of them has heeded the call of Maya Angelou, "If you're going to live, leave a legacy. Make a mark upon the world that can't be erased."

Jacqui You

Teresa entered my life as a free spirited nymph in a field of sunshine and light – a stark contrast to the rest of us desk-bound Zoom call attendees! I later learned she'd gifted herself her first surfing lesson as a birthday present – surfing being something I'd wanted to do for years. My interest was piqued and I instantly identified her as someone I'd like to meet. On a subsequent call, Teresa asked how others were keeping motivated so I grabbed my opportunity and private messaged her to ask if she'd like to connect.

We instantly hit it off and agreed to be accountability partners – a mixture of loving feedback, tough love, and challenging one another to think bigger, step out of our comfort zones, and test our wings as we both learn to fly higher and further. I'd had a dream for years of creating a community where people could hang out and be loved and celebrated for being their Authentic Selves – a safe space where we 'all got each other' no matter how weird or crazy others in our circles thought us. A home where we belong and can proudly fly our Freak flags high.

Sharing my dream with Teresa one Tuesday, she instantly challenged me to set up the first meeting for Friday – I agreed carried away by her enthusiasm. After the call I wondered how I could backtrack and get out of it. I couldn't and "Happi Friends!" was born.

"Happi Friends!" is a Tribe on a mission to uplift, inspire, and empower a Billion+ to live more joyful lives by being their Authentic Selves and spreading their unique brand of joy in the world. A place where dreams become reality – where we help, support, carry, share resources, and challenge each other as necessary. A Tribe that always has your back, believes in you and will remind you of your innate value and worth when you falter, as you fulfill your Destiny!

Jacqui You
jacqui@joyfully.me
www.facebook.com/groups/happifriendss

Salina Mahoney

I talked to Salina at a BBQ, shortly before Covid hit. She wore the coolest clothes I'd ever seen. They weren't fancy. They weren't expensive. They were just so HER. I came to find out she was an LA Stylist. A totally intimidating title but Salina was not intimidating at all. The tagline for her business, "So, I hear you're ready for a change?" As I got to know her, I discovered that transformation occurs on many levels. Her story of transformation and support for other people's evolving self is incredible. She is my "go-to" consultant for "what in the hell am I going to wear?" She helps me figure out how my "outside" can reflect my inside.

Here's her story.

My style journey began when I said *no* to something. I know, right? What good story starts with *no*? Well, mine does! A few years back, I had no idea how to dress. I was so lost; I didn't even know I *had* a problem. I wore a white, Hanes tee and black leggings (as pants, I might add) *every single day*. At that time in my life, I really didn't know who I was. I felt small and insignificant. I was surrounded by uninspiring relationships, with no idea what to pursue as a career and I struggled with an unfathomable amount of anxiety. I began to read fashion blogs online as my escape and that's when something within me started to awaken.

A little twinge in my gut wondered if I too, could be as... And I struggled to say it, even to myself because I found the word *so* cheesy and embarrassing but here it was: *fabulous*. The drama! Imagine me whispering: *Could I too, be fabulous?* Inspired, I made the decision to say «boy bye» to my black leggings. I had no idea what to replace them with but knew in my heart, they had to go. It seemed like such a small and insignificant choice. What I didn't realize is that the *real* choice I was making was *stepping out of my comfort zone*. Oomph. Not easy.

As I began to transform my style, I simultaneously began to uncover who I was. And I was happy to find that the reverse was also true: as I uncovered more of who I was, my sense of style bloomed. As I stepped into my power, I became an actual, real life stylist. I not only dressed myself well, but dressed *other* people well.

For like, my real job? Wild. And while dressing models for work is a blast, I'll never forget how it all started.

I know clothing is powerful. I believe we can use the power of dress to tell the world who we are, how we would like to be treated and where we're going. When we're not where we want to be just yet, style is a great place to start.

So, that's me. I know what it's like to feel stuck, unhappy and shy. I also know what it's like to not know where to begin. As your trusted wardrobe consultant, what I'm excited to share with you most are the simple tools needed to bloom from the wardrobe out.

And while you're here, whisper with me: I too, can be fabulous.

Salina Mahoney
www.Salinamahoney.com

KYM BELDEN

There is something amazing and beautiful in sharing someone's journey, in watching them ignite their joy and unleash their passion. The passion, the energy open and ready for more, the creation of positivity. This is what I live my life for, and what I have had the immense pleasure in sharing with Teresa. Except I didn't just share with her. Like a treasure, she shared the same... right back into my life.

We became accountability partners after both of us had previous partners that lacked lustre. Teresa and I meet every other week discussing our goals and what we accomplished from our previous phone call, possible dilemmas, insights, and what we want to further accomplish. We hold each other accountable for turning our thoughts into the actions of our life.

As a bio-mechanic, functional movement therapist, and sports and fitness performance consultant, I straighten and strengthen other people's bodies, creating balance so they can live happier, stronger, healthier lives. I work with their mindset to optimize current and future visions of themselves; where they are now, where they want to go and what they want to be like. Then the training begins.

The body and mind are interdependent, and weave a network of communication that your brain sends to your body, and your body sends to your brain. It is what dictates your performance, whatever that performance may be. And this body, mind exchange is happening every single second of every day. You can spend time lying on the couch, running marathons or somewhere in between. Whatever you choose to do, your physical and mental performance is constantly learning, being trained from your thoughts, your efforts and your actions. I leave you with this consideration: Why not make your performance something you can be happy with, pleased with when your head hits the pillow at the end of the day?

Assisting others in creating a life they enjoy, one of health, strength and purpose brings me complete joy. It is with this in mind that I dedicate my focus and kindness to enthusiastically support others toward positive change.

Kym Belden, C.H.E.K., USA Cycling
Physical Culture LLC
kymbelden@gmail.com

Charlotte Spivey

I first met Charlotte in a Writers Group. She matter-of-factly stated that she was a hypnotherapist and meditation guide. I thought, "Wow, you don't hear that everyday." Her voice, though, kept bringing me out of my thoughts and into a place of serenity. I thought, is she hypnotizing us right now? She's going to laugh when she reads this. That was definitely not her intention. We were, in fact, getting down to the business of reading and writing. As a show of support, I listened to one of her guided meditations and that was IT. I was like, damn, I can really meditate if this is the voice taking me there! Charlotte's meditations, and now, as the voice-over for much of my poetry online, are her gift to the world. Her story, like all my people, is nothing short of heroic.

MY PURPOSE

Charlotte writes:

My journey into hypnotherapy and meditation began with the need to be honest with myself. I had been struck down with mental illness and I hadn't told anyone the pain I was feeling. I kept it all to myself. I felt like a failure and even fifteen years ago, no one really spoke of mental illness. My illness was suffocating me, I was drowning in depression, anxiety and panic attacks. I felt lonely and frightened. In that moment of darkness, when I was laying on my rock bottom, I faced my fear and picked up the phone and spoke of my despair to someone. I realised then, that when you are honest, help will arrive. It may not be in the form you were expecting, mine was hypnotherapy, but it will arrive when you are ready.

My journey is now through working with those in need. I have been a hypnotherapist and meditation teacher for a decade, specialising in healing from depression, anxiety, and panic attacks. My hope is to guide those in search of their balance and healing, to find their internal worth, to show them that their answer is already within them. We hold the key to our happiness, but sometimes we are drawn so far away from ourselves, that we forget that everything we need, the answers that we are looking for, is already within our very own hands.

Excerpt from "The Real You" Guided Meditation available at www.white-willow.co.uk

...We forget to follow our dreams, we even forget to have them. Then we find ourselves one day, remembering our dreams and realising that we had forgotten. It's time to remember, we need you, life loves you. It's time for you to be who you really are...

Hear the full meditation at:
www.white-willow.co.uk/therealyou

Charlotte Spivey
Advanced Clinical and Medical Hypnotherapy
Specialist in long term co-morbid mental illness
www.white-willow.co.uk

Dishongh Scavo Barte

Dishongh is the visual force behind TeresaMartinINK. She is a well-seasoned Artist and my soul sister. I was scared to ask her for help on my projects — books, websites, media campaigns, and of course, reassembling my life one poem at a time. She jumped in without hesitation. And an incredible artistic collaboration unfolded. The writing, the pace, and the vision of this book would not have been achieved without her at every step of the way. Here's how she thinks about art, collaboration, and above all, life:

Ars Gratia Artis. (Art for art's sake) But is it? I believe it's for my sake and yours. Art doesn't happen in a void. We influence the artists and the artists influence us. To be part of something bigger than yourself keeps life in a healthy perspective. We are all part of this circle.

Enlightening, inspiring, encouraging, provocative, supportive, spiritual, sanctuary, disturbing, communal, peaceful. The list of gifts from the 'sake of art' is endless. Thankfully.

Believing in and being part of a project opens me to seeing ideas through someone else's lens, expanding personal understanding and perhaps evolving personal views. Flexibility is key, knowing that no one path is the answer. Remembering the most important goal is to take the first step and to continue to move forward.

I'm retired from years of Broadway, Film & TV work, as a Scenic Artist, Lighting Designer and Teacher. Now I am heavily involved with the visual Fine Arts with my creative partner. He has opened the door to writing that pairs with his paintings. The circle grows.

I have known Teresa from her first day of being. We shared so much when we were young. Then we both went out in the world, following nontraditional paths, making our own way. We are both much older now, a lot of life behind us. Triumphs and hard lessons learned and better for it. Now we are back in sync, like no time has passed. Famiglia Per Sempre

Dishongh Scavo Barte
GoodStudios@outlook.com
www.RandallMGood.com

•

MY PROCESS

•

Early readers of this work asked me critical questions:
How can we do this?
How can we leap into a life of love and joy?

I used poetry and prose as my "process" to reframe, reauthor, and ultimately repurpose my life. Hard questions arose during this process. Questions that I am still answering. I wanted to share those questions with you. Maybe you can uncover your answers late at night when all is quiet around you. Maybe you can uncover the answers alongside your people who support and strengthen you. Each question invites you into my process. Take what questions you want to answer and leave the rest. They will always be here.

1• One Woman told me over and over when I was young, "You are Strong. I see you. You can do this." This made all the difference. Who is that person for you? Are you that person for another woman or girl? Who could you be that person for and why would you pick her?

2 • Two Hands, working, will get your inner work done. Drawing, coloring, painting, sculpting, cooking, writing, sewing... There is true power in using my hands to clear my mind, to let my mind wander, to connect my mind to something outside my head. How do you use your two hands and what happens when you are engaged in creating something real? How much time can you give to this everyday? Why might that be important for you?

3 • Three deep long breaths, three times a day keeps me centered, refreshed. When I wake up, before eating my mid-day meal, and when I go to bed I take three long deep breaths and consciously think of nothing. I let my shoulders sink down, my face slack, and my reset button turns on. What guided meditations have worked for you? What helps you meditate? What makes it hard? What can you do to clear your mind?

4 • For You just because you are you. As my inner world shifted, I no longer felt that my outer clothes, hair, body language reflected me. Even my language began to change. Allowing others to show you unique jewelry, clothing, exercises, can be incredibly transforming. How can you ask your people to reflect back to you what they see, so that you can see yourself more clearly? How do you see yourself? How does another person see you? What is the difference and is it important?

5 • At least five, and perhaps more of you, will get together to talk, and talk, and talk. That's what we do, is it not? Regular, thoughtful, shared time together is critical. We are used to Zoom and meetup now, so use it to energize yourself. It's easy and convenient to gather folks from all over to share in this experience of transformation. Where would you look? Who would be those people? How can you nurture your community of like-minded spirits?

6 • Throughout the book, I reference books and people that have influenced my thinking. I have shared some of their most powerful words with you. These mantras and blessings, as I like to call them, got me through many rough spots this year. They also called upon me to work harder, be positive, and keep going. I thought you too, may want a bit of inspiration and to know who they are. You may even be inspired to pick up one of their readings. I strongly encourage it. It's like having a positive, supportive friend at the ready, even in the middle of the night when everyone is asleep. You can open their pages and know you are not alone. You have people. You are on the way. You are flying. What reading will you have at the "ready"?

7 • Dreams have guided me since I was a little girl living on Highland Lake in Illinois. I believed in the spirits who came to me in my dreams. I still do. What are your dreams telling you?

I leave you now, tucked in, under the covers, to Dream.

DREAMS IN SUMMER

For the young girls who listen to their dreams

The cool wet grass clippings clung to my ankles

walking through the backyard

at night, in summer.

The pungent smell of fresh cut lawns and tomato plants

explodes with the sparkle of a firefly

turning on, turning off.

In the night where lights stop, the Lake is there.

At the end of 14 feet of pier, feet feel the silky coolness

of the waters carrying sounds of a wedding band.

The creaking pier is smooth on the skin of a woman

who is reaching out,

into the backyard of life, into summer.

She looks into the deep blueish black of the water,

filled with whales, dinosaurs, and tigers from her dreams.

Behind her sits Chief White Feather.

Atop his white rock, looking out.

At the blueish black of the deep waters,

under him, in him, around him.

Take care,

of your dreams of summer, on Highland Lake.

About the Author • Teresa Martin

Teresa has been seeing patients since she was eight. Her grandfather, "Doc", gave her a white lab coat, stethoscope, and pen light and sent her into his exam rooms to take histories on his patients. She has taken herself very seriously ever since. She was awarded a full scholarship to nursing school and has been officially in the family business for the last dozen years. Over those years she's worked primarily in under-served, rural communities where health insurance and medical access were hard to come by. As a Women's Health Nurse, she once had a patient tell her, that she walked over two hundred miles to come to the clinic. The patient's shoes were well worn. She was eight months pregnant. She was smiling.

Before getting her RN license, Teresa was a therapist. Ninety percent of medicine was in the talking part so she figured that "therapist" was the logical place to start her career in healing. Her first job, right out of undergrad at Syracuse University, was as a volunteer for Hospice by the Bay in San Francisco during the AIDS epidemic in the 1990s. Her deep respect for the sacredness of each and every person and their right to full and complete access to medical care became deeply ingrained in her heart with each dying young man and woman she sat with. After completing additional undergraduate work at University of California, Berkeley, and then her Master of Science degree in Clinical Psychology at California State University, Fullerton, she published her thesis on the theory of mathematical models in decision-making with Cambridge University Press.

After graduate school, Teresa wanted to understand the big picture in healthcare, to see how "the system" worked, or didn't. She worked in philanthropy trying hard to see where the dollars came from, went to, and were spent on, in health care. She knew it would shake her grandfather, "Doc", to his knees. He believed in providing care without consideration of insurance. He saw patients at their home and accepted "trade" for services rendered in the form of fishing rods and baked goods. Her naivete of the business of healthcare gone, she knew it was time to get back to being boots on the ground. She needed to work for people who walked hundreds of miles, just to see a Doctor.

Nursing in Women's Health, Labor&Delivery, and eventually managing clinics as an Associate Director of Nursing, showed Teresa she could use her education, experience, and dedication to serve, to make life and death differences for others, right here, right now. She decided it was time to see the full spectrum of medicine. She shifted her practice to geriatrics, dementia, Hospice, and Palliative care. Caring for the elderly and dying brought much emotional growth and awe to her practice. However, as Covid seeped into our vernacular, she found the work was becoming her kryptonite. She left for a short stint to rejuvenate, but returned, to work again on the frontlines as an inpatient Palliative Care Nurse at her local hospital.

Her rejuvenation period allowed her to go inward and find answers to the questions haunting many of us during Covid – do I want to be a nurse? If so, how am I going to mentally prepare better for the volume and kind of death we are processing on the frontlines? How can I help other frontline workers get real rejuvenation time? During her months off, Teresa wrote two books and began the seed of her next venture, TeresaMartinINK. A for-purpose company dedicated to collaborating with nurses, nursing institutions, and community front line workers to ask the hard questions about "self-care" during Covid and share practices that are shown to work. She recently shared some of the work she's done both in the written word and through TeresaMartinINK at the Mental Health Association of San Francisco's conference, "Redefining Crazy: It's the System, not the People." Her full interview can be seen on her website at TeresaMartinINK.com.

Somewhere in all of this, Teresa birthed two beautiful boys who are almost men now. When they moved from the big city in California to rural New Mexico and then on to rural North Carolina, Teresa was dissatisfied with the children's books available to her boys on moving. So, she wrote her own book, dedicated to her two boys that had to move around the country with her. The book, *Big Ernie's New Home*, was published by the American Psychological Association and won the iparenting award and has been translated into Korean.

Her partner of over thirty years asked her on their first date, "what do you want to be?". Without hesitation, she replied, "a writer". He replied, "Cool, I'll illustrate the books for you then". And that was that. They continue to share an office and collaborate on the books she thinks need writing – the books she can't find anywhere. This first volume in this series, is what she desperately needed to know during her time away from nursing, "what does it really look like, from the first person, to change your life?" What she found was the process that worked for her to change her life and leap into the life of love and joy of her choosing. She has given you her gift of vulnerability, so that you may become more comfortable with your own. So that you, too, may leap into your life of love and joy.

ABOUT THE ILLUSTRATOR • WHITNEY MARTIN

Storyboard Artist, Illustrator, Designer, and Firefighter

Whitney Bruce Martin started drawing before he could even write his name. His Christmas letters to Santa featured every item on his list, all meticulously hand drawn to scale without a single word on the page. Whitney worked full-time to put himself through both his undergraduate program in illustration and master's program in art & design with a concentration in animation, all the while devoting his time on the weekends as a Reservist Marine. Whitney jokes about how he would take off the beret to lace up his boots.

Whitney began his career in animation at Walt Disney Feature Animation back when "the mouse" recruited college kids and sent them to Florida to work in the fishbowl, for tourists to gawk at, while they scratched out hand drawn animation cells. He stayed at Disney Feature for five years working on *The Hunchback of Notre Dame, Hercules, Pocahontas, Tarzan,* and *Mulan.* He moved on to *King of the Hill* — harkening back to his Texas roots. Story-boarding on the cult classic gave him an appreciation for a damn good story. Whitney expanded his talents into the children's book world and illustrated over a dozen books for Simon & Schuster, Holiday House, and Magination Press.

Whitney took a short break from animation to become a firefighter. Most people don't have the opportunity to pursue two different passions in their lifetime, but he went for it. Becoming a firefighter, firefighting instructor, and "one of the guys" will remain one of his most sacred experiences. Whitney has since retired his helmet and boots, and now wears his beret full-time.

Most recently, he has worked in the animated TV circuit at DreamWorks, Universal Studios, and Bento Box working on *Boss Baby, Curious George, Housebroken,* and *Bob's Burgers* respectively. He started his own YouTube channel, "Frame by Frame", to encourage storyboard artists to come together to analyze story sequences and learn from one another. His fellow firefighters nicknamed him Martin "The Machine", an apt description of his work ethic, leadership, and drive to excel. It also speaks to his quirky sense of humor that only a Texan who's worked on *King of the Hill* would have.

www.wbmartinart.com
www.linkedin.com/in/wbmartin1

ACKNOWLEDGMENTS

I would never have listened to my inner voice to publish a first-person narrative about my transformational journey without the complete confidence and support of my partner, Whitney. The way you just look at me and say, "of course you can write the book honey, you write from the heart." You give me the courage to keep typing.

My colorful road of transformation has been blessed with many souls to thank for their support. I am so blessed to have you in my life. Thanks to Sabrina Mahoney and her clan – you are my first and most righteous mastermind group. Our Sunday night dinners around the pool talking "art" has elevated my identity to one of "artist." A feat I could not have achieved without your encouragement and confidence in me. Thanks to Happi Friends – you guys are supportive in ways that only a group of "transforming folk" can be. How marvelous to gather with like-minded souls twice a month and share our successes and challenges of our passion projects. I can't wait to meet up in Kathmandu in '22. Thanks to my inner circle of soul sisters. Dishongh, you have given me the beautiful interior of this book and your soulful reflections over the last few months. Our collaborative process in the "making of" has been a process of pure joy and healing. The pages here would not exist without your unwavering support and guiding hands.

For ALL my soul sisters and brothers, and I am blessed with too many to name:

I owe you a trip to the wine country – invites coming. I can't wait to toast you with "Cent'anni." Special thanks to my accountability partners, beta readers, stylists, media coaches, editors, voiceovers, web designers, videographers, publisher, and dreamers, that are a part of my inner circles personally and/or professionally. You all helped make this happen. Inside me, and, on the page.

COME FLY WITH US

Join Our Community
of Readers, Writers, and Dreamers

Community is critical.
Our "people" give us the nourishment
to rise and the fire to keep going.

Join our community of like-minded writers, readers, and community of people transforming into our best selves. Be the first to hear about our goings-on, new reads, and community events.

www.TeresaMartinINK.com

GERTIE'S GUIDE
The lessons and legacy of women caring for one another

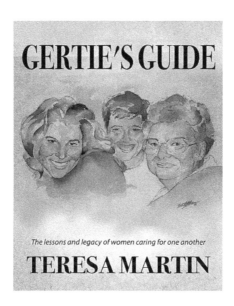

Who will recognize how resilient and striking are the millions of women who are "aging"? Women will recognize these women. Daughters, neighbors, sisters, nurses, caregivers, housekeepers, medical technicians, Doctors, pharmacists. The list of women who will care for these women goes on and on.

It is not a burden we carry. It is the single most important opportunity we have to exercise our power as women.